Ed Shaw is Pastor of Emmanuel City Centre Church, Bristol, UK and Ministry Director at www.livingout.org. He has written widely, authoring numerous blogs and articles as well as the bestselling books, *The Plausibility Problem* and *Purposeful Sexuality*. Ed loves family and friends, church and city, gin and tonic, music and books.

THE INTIMACY DEFICIT

INTER-VARSITY PRESS
SPCK Group, Studio 101, The Record Hall, 16–16A Baldwin's Gardens, London
EC1N 7RJ, England
Email: ivp@ivpbooks.com
Website: www.ivpbooks.com

© Ed Shaw, 2025

Ed Shaw has asserted his right under the Copyright, Designs and Patents Act 1988 to be identified as Author of this work.

All rights reserved. No part of this publication may be reproduced, stored in a retrieval system, or transmitted, in any form or by any means, electronic, mechanical, photocopying, recording or otherwise, without the prior permission of the publisher or the Copyright Licensing Agency.

Unless otherwise indicated scripture quotations are taken from The Holy Bible, New International Version (Anglicized edition). Copyright © 1979, 1984, 2011 by Biblica. Used by permission of Hodder & Stoughton Ltd, an Hachette UK company. All rights reserved. 'NIV' is a registered trademark of Biblica. UK trademark number 1448790.
Scripture quotations marked MSG are taken from *THE MESSAGE*, copyright © 1993, 2002, 2018 by Eugene H. Peterson. Used by permission of NavPress. All rights reserved. Represented by Tyndale House Publishers, Inc.
p. 2: From *Physical* by Andrew McMillan published by Jonathan Cape. Copyright © Andrew McMillan, 2015. Reprinted by permission of The Random House Group Limited.
p. 38: *Mere Christianity* by C.S. Lewis copyright © 1942, 1943, 1944, 1952 C.S. Lewis Pte. Ltd. Extract reprinted by permission.
p. 81: *The Weight of Glory* by C.S. Lewis copyright © 1949 C.S. Lewis Pte. Ltd. Extract reprinted by permission.
p. 87: 'Horae Canonicae: Sext' copyright © 1955 by The Estate of W.H. Auden. Reprinted by permission of Curtis Brown, Ltd. All rights reserved.

First published 2025

British Library Cataloguing-in-Publication Data
A catalogue record for this book is available from the British Library.

ISBN: 978–1–78359–948–6
eBook ISBN: 978–1–78359–949–3

Set in Minion Pro 11/14 pt
Typeset by Fakenham Prepress Solutions
Printed in Great Britain by Ashford Colour Press Ltd, Gosport, Hampshire

Produced on paper from sustainable forests

Inter-Varsity Press publishes Christian books that are true to the Bible and that communicate the gospel, develop discipleship and strengthen the church for its mission in the world.

IVP originated within the Inter-Varsity Fellowship, now the Universities and Colleges Christian Fellowship, a student movement connecting Christian Unions in universities and colleges throughout Great Britain, and a member movement of the International Fellowship of Evangelical Students. Website: www.uccf.org.uk. That historic association is maintained, and all senior IVP staff and committee members subscribe to the UCCF Basis of Faith.

'In an age of chronic disconnection, Ed carefully pastors the reader through a journey that is refreshingly honest, grounded and hopeful. His insights help us discern the intimacy gaps in our own lives and equip us with practical steps towards truly living life in all its fullness.'
Ruth Bushyager, Bishop of Horsham

'Ed puts his finger on what our parched and fragmented hearts are desperately yearning for. It's an achingly beautiful picture of flourishing humanity. And how practically, even today, I can enjoy a deeper sense of being at home with God in his world, in my own skin and with others.'
Mark Ellis, CEO, Keswick Ministries

'The kindness and rawness of Ed's writing permeates every page. We each long to be known and loved – Ed invites us to have that desire satisfied in and through Jesus. Practical, real, honest and hope-filled; this book is essential reading for anyone who has wanted better or deeper relationships.'
Jo Frost, author and Director of Communications and Engagement, Evangelical Alliance

'I often come across books that someone claims are essential, life-changing or a much-needed correction in our contemporary culture. I have a pile of them mostly unread. But this book is all those and more. It has already changed me, and I commend it to you as a thing of great wisdom, humility, learning and grace. Its greatest strength for me has been to draw together four different strands of intimacy (with God, ourselves, others and creation) rather than insist on one as all-important, treating each simply, briefly, movingly and practically. There are so many things here that need saying, but which I hadn't managed to think yet, and Ed expresses them beautifully. I feel deeply encouraged and gently challenged to discover more of the intimacies God has made me for, that I might exult in a fuller, richer life. Thank you, Ed. I have a feeling this is the book I shall be commending to

students I teach, and to friends and family I love, for some time to come.'
Andrew Nicholls, Director of Pastoral Care, Oak Hill College, London

'In this pastorally warm and spiritually enriching book, Ed Shaw reminds us that our great longing as human beings is for intimacy. This is not about sex, but our need to be connected with God, ourselves, others and the creation. Rooted in compelling biblical teaching, and written with the wisdom acquired from decades of ministry, he helps us understand what it means to enjoy intimacy, the barriers that undermine intimacy and steps that we can take to foster greater intimacy. It is concise and accessible, poetic and moving, and will encourage readers to seek greater fullness in all their relationships as they experience the blessings of their new life in Christ.'
John Stevens, National Director, FIEC

'Ed Shaw successfully and powerfully reclaims the concept of intimacy and restores it within a thoroughly biblical and wonderfully pastoral framework. It is widely researched and winsomely applied, but what sets it apart is his vulnerability, authenticity and humour. *The Intimacy Deficit* is a deeply disarming and enormously edifying read.'
Jago Wynne, Rector of Holy Trinity Clapham, London

THE INTIMACY DEFICIT

Fully Enjoying God, Yourself,
Others and Creation

Ed Shaw

We all grew up in one moral ecology or another. We all create microcultures around us by the way we live our lives and the vibes we send out to those around us. One of the greatest legacies a person can leave is a moral ecology – a system of belief and behaviour that lives on after they die.
David Brooks

This book is a loving celebration of my honorary aunt, Ruth Kisch (1943–2024), who permeates its pages.

And it's for my nieces, Martha, Eliza and Ada, and nephews, Seth and Walter.

This is Uncle Ed's ecology of belief and behaviour, passed on with all my love and prayers.

Contents

Introduction: the intimacy deficit   1

1 Intimacy with God   8
2 Enjoying intimacy with God   18
3 Intimacy with yourself   32
4 Enjoying intimacy with yourself   43
5 Intimacy with others   56
6 Enjoying intimacy with others   67
7 Intimacy with creation   79
8 Enjoying intimacy with creation   89

Conclusion: an intimacy audit   101

Acknowledgements   111

Introduction: the intimacy deficit

> Man – of all ages and cultures – is confronted with the solution of one and the same question: the question of how to overcome separateness, how to achieve union, how to transcend one's own individual life and find at-onement.[1]
> *Erich Fromm*

Rescuing the concept

This is not a book about sexuality and/or sex. That might be a relief: they might have scarred you, or they might just bore you. If that's a disappointment, the good news is that I've already written two books on those subjects.[2] Instead, this book is more important and perhaps more controversial than anything to do with sex: its main point is that your greatest need in life is intimacy, a sense of oneness and connectedness both outside of yourself and with yourself, but *not* of the sexual kind. As psychologist Erich Fromm argues above, this is true of you whoever you are, wherever you come from. We all have what I'm calling an 'intimacy deficit'. If you want to enjoy your life on this planet (and beyond), you should read on and find out how it can be filled.

The problem is that when we hear the word 'intimacy', we tend to think of sex and sexual relationships immediately, and we are likely to presume that a book entitled *The Intimacy Deficit* is going to be about a lack of sex. Sex is where true intimacy is apparently to be found in today's Western world. The contemporary poet Andrew McMillan demonstrates this attitude when he writes:

---

1 Erich Fromm, *The Art of Loving* (London: Thorsons, 1995), p. 8.
2 Ed Shaw, *The Plausibility Problem: The Church and Same-sex Attraction* (London: IVP UK, 2015); Ed Shaw, *Purposeful Sexuality: A Short Introduction* (London: IVP UK, 2021).

Introduction

> intimacy which means knowing
> the exact taste of someone else's
> sleep in their mouth on waking[3]

That definition manages to be both wonderfully off-putting and helpfully illustrative of contemporary attitudes. He is accurately reflecting where our society says that true intimacy is experienced: in bed with someone else. Talk of enjoying an 'intimate relationship' is so often a euphemism for a sexually active one.[4]

Of course, that experience, that taste, *is* intimate: it's about becoming one with another person and connecting deeply with them. But to tie intimacy to sex and sex alone is harmful. It creates an intimacy deficit for anyone not smelling someone else's bad breath first thing in the morning (which, put like that, they might not mind) and dangerously limits the contexts in which people seek to find it. My friend Nate Collins rightly points out that, 'The concept of intimacy has been, like so many other social goods, cannibalized by sexuality',[5] and I think that a generation or two of us bear the scars.

This book seeks to rescue intimacy from just the bedroom and show how it can and should be experienced by all of us, all over the place, in a range of non-sexual and yet beautifully intimate relationships with God, with yourself, with others and with creation. This is so important because, as we'll discover, we were created to need intimacy in each of these four key areas. Without enjoying it in each of them, we are going to struggle to enjoy the life of fullness that we were created for. This is true whether you're reading these words as a deeply committed Christian, a very wobbly one, or someone who is not yet a Christian. I'm writing for all of you

---

[3] Andrew McMillan, 'protest of the physical', in *Physical* (London: Jonathan Cape, 2015), p. 32.
[4] Just one example from when I was writing this book can be found here: Jasper Jolly, 'BP staff risk sack if they fail to disclose intimate relationships with colleagues', *The Guardian*, 10 June 2024, https://www.theguardian.com/business/article/2024/jun/10/bp-staff-risk-sack-if-they-fail-to-disclose-intimate-relationships-with-colleagues.
[5] Nate Collins, *All But Invisible: Exploring Identity Questions at the Intersection of Faith, Gender & Sexuality* (Grand Rapids, MI: Zondervan, 2017), p. 157.

and myself, because I need just as much help to grasp all of this as you do.

Defining true intimacy

So, if intimacy doesn't just equal sex, how do we better understand it? Over the past decade or so, I've been reading as widely as possible on the concept, and I think that the writer Giovanni Frazzetto helps us to get there when he suggests that, 'Intimacy means to enact, rehearse and polish modes of connection.'[6] This is the sort of wider and deeper definition of intimacy we need, which might include sex but helpfully broadens it to something that can be enjoyed in numerous different ways and contexts – connecting, for instance, with our Creator, with ourselves, with other people and with the world around us.

My working definition of intimacy would edit this down still further to just three words: *oneness through connection*. An alternative summary could be *fullness through relationship*. Both helpfully communicate a reality as well as a feeling (a sense of oneness or fullness) that is achieved and experienced through interaction (connectedness to or a relationship with) someone or something. This is the sort of intimacy we'll explore in the rest of the book, with plenty of worked examples, as we seek to solve the intimacy deficit by enacting, rehearsing and polishing our modes of connection in four key areas of life.

But at this stage, you might like just one example of this sort of non-sexual intimacy, this oneness through connection, in the real world. If so, I think that the best place to point you is the most intimate, deepest, longest-lasting relationship of them all: the one enjoyed eternally by God the Father and his Son Jesus Christ. And perhaps the best insight into the intimacy they have is the prayer time Jesus enjoys with his Father on the night before he knows that he will die on the cross, preserved for us in John 17.

---

6 Giovanni Frazzetto, *Together, Closer: Stories of Intimacy in Friendship, Love, and Family* (London: Piatkus, 2017), p. 31.

Introduction

Have a listen in as Jesus talks openly and honestly to his Father on that dreadful night. Remarkably, he spends some of his last precious moments before his arrest and crucifixion talking to God about people who will become his followers through the future witness of his very first disciples. He is praying for you and me, and his words are the greatest expression of true intimacy I've ever come across:

> My prayer is not for them alone. I pray also for those who will believe in me through their message, that all of them may be one, Father, just as you are in me and I am in you. May they also be in us so that the world may believe that you have sent me.
> (John 17:20–21)

Why is this such a good, living and breathing, example of intimacy? Notice how Jesus describes his relationship with his Father. They are so close, so connected, that although they are still separate persons, they are inseparable, 'in' each other always. You can't get any more intimate than that. If you want examples of this intimacy – oneness through connection – just think about the ways they relate to one another throughout the eyewitness accounts of Matthew, Mark, Luke and John: the time they spend with each other, what they say about each other, everything they do together and the love they both constantly demonstrate for each other.

But in this introduction, it's also worth noticing that it's – incredibly – this sort of oneness, connectedness and intimacy that Jesus wants us to enjoy with each other and with him and his Father. His prayer is 'that all of them may be one, Father, just as you are in me and I am in you. May they also be in us'. Jesus is talking about his oneness with his Father God not to teach a theological reality but to ask that this might become a felt reality for us too – that we might become one, connected to and intimate with him, his Father in heaven *and* our fellow Christians from all times and places. This is the intimacy that we were most created to enjoy, that we need. This is the sort of intimacy we'll explore for the rest of this book.

Exploring the deficit

Talk of feeling at one with God and with other people will instantly make many of us feel the painful lack of such feelings much of the time. This book has been written to name that deficit and to begin to reduce it, so keep reading – especially because it's my belief that this intimacy deficit is at the heart of so many of the problems present in our lives and the lives of those around us today.

My main role in life is as a pastor, and I've now been serving as one for over a quarter of a century. Over that time, I've been slowly learning that all the big problems people have kindly entrusted me with – their broken relationships, their painful loneliness, their powerful addictions, their crippling anxieties – are nearly always down to an intimacy deficit in their lives: a lack of closeness, oneness and connectedness to God, themselves, others or creation.

I learned this most powerfully through pastoring someone I'll call Percy (because hardly anyone is called Percy today). A year into our friendship, he was open about an addiction to pornography, which was crippling him. As I sought to help him to battle his addiction, we noticed that when he was rightly enjoying intimacy in the four contexts we'll explore in the rest of this book, the false intimacy of pornography had much less of a hold on his life. At the same time, I was noticing the same with my different struggles: they were lessened when I was enjoying a sense of real connectedness, a oneness with God, myself, others and creation. I now use this 'Intimacy Audit' regularly in my pastoral care of others (and my self-care). I'll share it at the end of the book.

Of course, noticing this connection, those contexts, was no unique breakthrough or insight. The importance of intimacy (widely defined) in those areas has been noticed by others, non-Christian and Christian alike. One of the most helpful secular books I've read on addiction sees therapist Craig Nakken observe that, 'Addiction is an emotional relationship with an object or event, through which addicts try to meet their needs for intimacy.'[7] The author of the most helpful Christian book on pornography I've read, psychologist William Struthers, writes that,

> A starving man will eat anything that is put before him. An intimacy-neglected man will grasp at any available opportunity to know or be known. The need for intimacy will build without emotional connection, and he will look for this connection in unhealthy and unproductive places.[8]

It is not just our addictions that are the result of the intimacy deficit in our lives. Christian psychiatrist Curt Thompson goes as far as to say that, 'All sin, all idolatry, all coping strategies in which I indulge are ways for me to satiate my hunger for relationship, my longing to be known and loved, my desire to be desired.'[9] This is an important observation. Too often, Christians just repent of their sins and the harm they do to God, ourselves, others and creation without any real understanding of how we can, with God's help, change our circumstances in ways that will effectively stop us from quickly returning to them. We fail to see the deep, right needs for connection behind them and just try to go cold turkey rather than seeking to meet our God-given desires for intimacy in God-given ways. We simply resolve to stop thinking or doing something negative and harmful without replacing it with something good and positive, which nearly always means that the old damaging habits return to refill the gap.

This book seeks to begin to change that – for addicts like Percy and for all of us in our different struggles – working on the premise that the root cause of so many of our harmful patterns of thought and behaviour is our intimacy deficit.

---

[7] Craig Nakken, *The Addictive Personality: Understanding the Addictive Process and Compulsive Behavior* (Danvers, MA: Hazelden, 1996), p. 8.

[8] William M. Struthers, *Wired for Intimacy: How Pornography Hijacks the Male Brain* (San Francisco, CA: IVP USA, 2009), p. 160.

[9] Curt Thompson, *The Soul of Shame: Retelling the Stories We Believe about Ourselves* (San Francisco, CA: IVP USA, 2015), p. 105.

A beginner's guide

We're going to examine what I see as the four main God-given contexts for intimacy in turn, with chapters setting out the biblical cases for them, each followed by a chapter that seeks to help us to *begin* to enjoy that experience of intimacy more and more in our daily lives. This book is just a primer, an introduction. But in one another's company, benefitting from the wisdom God has given many secular writers and professionals, enjoying the insights of other Christians down the ages and – most of all – empowered by God's Spirit speaking and acting through God's word, the hope and prayer is that we'll start to learn how to lessen the intimacy deficit that's stopping us from enjoying the life Jesus wants us to experience. For, as he once memorably said, 'I have come that they may have life, and have it to the full' (John 10:10).

1
Intimacy with God

> We cannot experience the fullness of intimacy until we understand that it goes deeper than anything we might find in the greatest human encounter, until we realize that its origins lie far beyond ourselves, or our universe, to the very creator.[1]
> Elaine Storkey

Father and child reunion

Think for a moment of the last time you saw a loving father caring for his child. I hope that it wasn't too long ago (while recognising that, for some, it was tragically something you never experienced yourself). I can think of plenty of examples from just last Sunday as my church family gathered: a new dad cautiously burping his newborn daughter, another taking his crying child out for a walk, still another scooping his toddler up in a loving embrace.

A good father–child relationship is one of the most repeated biblical pictures we are given of the intimate relationship we were created to enjoy with the one Jesus tells us we get to call 'Our Father in heaven' (Matthew 6:9). The first appearance of this picture is in the Old Testament, where God portrays himself as a father to communicate the intimate nature of the love and care he has shown to his chosen people, the nation of Israel. Here is just one example:

> When Israel was a child, I loved him,
>   and out of Egypt I called my son.

---

[1] Elaine Storkey, *The Search for Intimacy* (London: Hodder & Stoughton, 1995), p. 70.

> But the more they were called,
>   the more they went away from me.
> They sacrificed to the Baals
>   and they burned incense to images.
> It was I who taught Ephraim to walk,
>   taking them by the arms;
> but they did not realise
>   it was I who healed them.
> I led them with cords of human kindness,
>   with ties of love.
> To them I was like one who lifts
>   a little child to the cheek,
>   and I bent down to feed them.
>
> (Hosea 11:1-4)

Spend a second or two picturing a loving dad with his arms outstretched to catch a child performing their first stumbling steps, him embracing them cheek to cheek when they have fallen and the tears are flowing, him kneeling to give them food to motivate them to keep going. This is how God has, and always will, relate to us – his people – even in our sin. His arms are outstretched when we stumble. He holds us to his cheek when we fall. He reaches down to feed us the spiritual food we need to sustain us. He is connected to us, and we are connected to him, in those deeply intimate sorts of ways.

Jesus, of course, underlines all of this in one of his most famous parables, which tells the tale of a prodigal son. This son, like the Old Testament nation of Israel, has left his father behind and sought to meet his intimacy needs in relationships with other people or things. But as his search fails, he miraculously remembers his father's generous provision for even his servants and resolves to head home and join them. We then read what the novelist Tobias Wolff has rightly described as 'the most beautiful words ever written or said':[2]

---

2 Tobias Wolff, *Old School* (London: Bloomsbury, 2005), p. 195.

> But while he was still a long way off, his father saw him and was filled with compassion for him; he ran to his son, threw his arms around him and kissed him.
> (Luke 15:20)

This father and child reunion is one of the most intimate moments in the whole of Scripture: a selfish child enthusiastically loved and embraced by the father he had enthusiastically rejected and run away from. Moments before, they were divided by the son's costly betrayal. The very next, they were reunited by the father's extravagant forgiveness.

The Roman Catholic priest Henri Nouwen always struggled to feel the father love of God until he saw this moment captured by the Dutch artist Rembrandt in the famous painting *The Return of the Prodigal Son*. Why not pause and have a look for yourself? But whether or not this picture (or the wider story) connects with you, the reality is that this is not just a picture or parable; this sort of loving embrace is the spiritual reality whenever any of us return home to our Father God, recognising that we've got nowhere without him. Becoming a Christian simply involves turning back to him and then being swept up in his arms as he runs to meet you. Living the Christian life sees this process repeated. However many times you find yourself setting out on the journey home, this is *always* the sort of welcome you'll receive. I love how the Christian philosopher James K. A. Smith explains and applies it:

> At the heart of the madness of the gospel is an almost unbelievable mystery that speaks to a deep human hunger only intensified by a generation of broken homes: to be seen and known and loved by a father. Maybe navigating the tragedy and heartbreak of this fallen world is realizing this hunger might not be met by the ones we expect or hope will come looking for us, but then meeting a Father who adopts you, who chooses you, who sees you a long way off and comes running and says 'I've been waiting for you.'[3]

---

3 James K. A. Smith, *On the Road with Saint Augustine: A Real-World Spirituality for Restless Hearts* (Ada, MI: Brazos, 2019), p. 201.

Don't those words help you to feel connected to God, wanted by him? Your Father God is waiting for *you*. He is running to meet *you* and bring you *home*. If you struggle to feel that connection, why not pray for God's Spirit to help you to feel the reality of God's fatherly love and care for you? According to the apostle Paul in Romans 8:14–16, the Holy Spirit brought about your adoption as God's child and empowers us both to cry out to him as our Father and to know that we are his children. God's Spirit is the divine agent of intimacy with God in our lives, enabling the connections we often struggle to make by ourselves. This is just one of the biblical ways he seeks to communicate the sort of intimate relationship God offers us all in Jesus.

You've got a friend

'Do you want to be my friend?' is a question we might not have been asked since the school playground (or maybe not even then), but it's also a question the Creator God of the universe poses to each one of us. It's another way in which he communicates the sort of deeply connected or intimate relationship he wants with us.

Again, we see this in the Old and New Testaments. In a prayer to God recorded in the history book of 2 Chronicles, the Old Testament patriarch Abraham is called 'Abraham your friend' (2 Chronicles 20:7). Later, God himself, speaking through his prophet Isaiah, uses the same language, describing his people as 'you descendants of Abraham my friend' (Isaiah 41:8). These references serve to remind us of the close relationship Abraham and God enjoyed – how they talked with each other, how God provided for Abraham and how Abraham (most of the time) took God at his word. Friendship is an accurate way of describing their close connection, even though it was one between the Creator and one of his creatures.

Jesus takes this talk of human friendship with God and runs with it, fleshing it out. In the intimate setting of the Last Supper with his closest disciples on the night before his death, he speaks these words:

> Greater love has no one than this: to lay down one's life for one's friends. You are my friends if you do what I command. I no longer call you servants, because a servant does not know his master's business. Instead, I have called you friends, for everything that I learned from my Father I have made known to you.
> (John 15:13–15)

My favourite definition of friendship is pastor Tim Keller's: 'There are two features of real friendship – constancy and transparency. Real friends always let you in, and they never let you down.'[4] In these verses, Jesus demonstrates both his constant love – in his willingness to even die for them – and his transparent openness – in having shared everything with them. Jesus did not just use the language of friendship; he lived the reality of friendship. I recently worked my way through John's Gospel and listed all the ingredients of the sort of deep, intimate friendship Jesus offered his first disciples: initiative-taking, challenge, time, fun, self-disclosure, tears, service, patience, comfort, loyalty, love, honesty, sensitivity, prayer, forgiveness and hospitality. He displays them all – and more.

A potential response in us today is to be jealous of those disciples who heard these words and experienced these realities in the flesh. Although we might, every so often, sing the hymn 'What a Friend We Have in Jesus', we struggle to feel the reality when we cannot see and hear him in person. But recently, I've come to appreciate what a benefit it is to have a Jesus who is truly my friend, who has laid down his life for me too, who has shared everything with me, but who is not visibly, physically present with me. There are places where I cannot take a normal friend – like inside the MRI machine, into the job interview or with me into a prison cell. But, through his Spirit, my friend Jesus can still be by my side in each of those scary locations and in any others too. This, I think, is one of the reasons Jesus told his friends that his Spirit's presence within them

---

4 Timothy Keller with Kathy Keller, *The Meaning of Marriage: Facing the Complexities of Marriage with the Wisdom of God* (London: Hodder & Stoughton, 2011), p. 112.

was better than his bodily presence with them (see John 16:7): it was only with the Spirit of Jesus living inside them that they'd never walk alone. Some words from the Anglican Bishop J. C. Ryle have often helped me to feel the joy of this reality:

> The Lord Jesus *goes with His friends wherever they go.* There is no possible separation between Him and those whom He loves. There is no place or position on earth, or under the earth, that can divide them from the great Friend of their souls. When the path of duty calls them far away from home, He is their companion; when they pass through the fire and water of fierce tribulation, He is with them; when they lie down on the bed of sickness, He stands by them and makes their trouble work for good; when they go down the valley of the shadow of death, and friends and relatives stand still and can go no further, He goes by their side. When they wake up in the unknown world of Paradise, they are still with Him; when they rise with a new body at the judgment day, they will not be alone. He will own them for His friends, and say, 'They are mine: deliver them and let them go free.' He will make good His own words: 'I am with you always, even unto the end of the world' (Matthew 28:20).[5]

That is the quality, the constancy, of friendship that only Jesus can give us by his Spirit, and that is what he freely offers all of us today.

As a result, we should dare to describe ourselves as friends of God, as those who are closely connected to him. That title doesn't just belong to Abraham; it can be said of you too, if you are a Christian. We should picture him by our side in all times and places because that is exactly where he always is.

One of my favourite hymns is John Ireland's beautiful setting of the puritan Samuel Crossman's poem 'My Song is Love Unknown'. It's often sung at Easter. Having spent verses describing the love of Jesus demonstrated in his birth, life and death, Crossman ends with

---

5 J. C. Ryle, *Practical Religion* (Edinburgh: Banner of Truth, 1998), p. 348.

these deeply personal, intimate words describing where everything Jesus has done wonderfully leaves us:

> This is my Friend,
> in Whose sweet praise
> I all my days
> could gladly spend.

We all need to sing of, feel and live out this reality more: that you've – I've – got a friend in him. If you would struggle to sing these words today, pray for the Spirit of Jesus to help you to feel the presence of your friend Jesus more tomorrow.

Can't take my eyes off you

The intimacy we get to enjoy with God can be compared with a perfect father and child relationship, to the best of all friendships, but it's also portrayed in Scripture as the greatest romantic relationship of them all.

This reality permeates the whole of the Scriptures. In the Old Testament, it's most prominent in the love duet between God and his people that is Song of Songs, but we also see it explored by prophets like Isaiah. He records God saying to Israel:

> As a young man marries a young woman,
>   so will your Builder marry you;
> as a bridegroom rejoices over his bride,
>   so will your God rejoice over you.
> (Isaiah 62:5)

Here, God is comparing his relationship with his people to the most obviously intimate relationship of them all: a marriage between a man and a woman and the joy of their physical sexual union.

I don't know whether you've ever been to a wedding where the groom can't take his eyes off his bride, and where his speech has left no one in any doubt about his joy in being united to her in

Intimacy with God

marriage. You might (depending on your personality and circumstances) have found the experience charming or nauseating, but what you were seeing and hearing was just a small insight into how God relates to his people. He can't take his eyes off us. Even millennia before his wedding day he is, here in Isaiah, predicting the joy he will feel when his love for us is finally consummated.

That day is coming soon, according to the New Testament. We're repeatedly told that Jesus is the divine bridegroom, his church is his bride, and human history will end with their wedding:

> Then I saw 'a new heaven and a new earth,' for the first heaven and the first earth had passed away, and there was no longer any sea. I saw the Holy City, the new Jerusalem, coming down out of heaven from God, prepared as a bride beautifully dressed for her husband. And I heard a loud voice from the throne saying, 'Look! God's dwelling-place is now among the people, and he will dwell with them. They will be his people, and God himself will be with them and be their God. "He will wipe every tear from their eyes. There will be no more death" or mourning or crying or pain, for the old order of things has passed away.'
> (Revelation 21:1–4)

Soon and very soon, God's people from all times and places will get married to God's Son Jesus and live happily ever after. We will look stunning for him, and he will rejoice in our beauty. Heaven and earth will come together, and God himself will live with his people in a world made new, a state of perfection that will continue forever and a day.

All of this is why author Rebecca McLaughlin can describe marriage in the here and now as 'a gateway drug to a far more fulfilling relationship'.[6] It's just a foretaste, a trailer for something much more

---

6 Rebecca McLaughlin, *Confronting Christianity: 12 Hard Questions for the World's Largest Religion* (Wheaton, IL: Crossway, 2019), p. 161.

satisfying that is open to all: being united, connected and made one with God in Christ for eternity.

To help us to look forward to the perfect intimacy of this day more and more, we need to develop the sort of biblical imagination that our spiritual forebears had in spades. Here is the eighteenth-century preacher Jonathan Edwards riffing on what Scripture tells us to look forward to:

> There will come the time, when Christ will sweetly invite his spouse to enter with him into the palace of his glory, which he had been preparing for her from the foundation of the world, and he shall as it were take her by the hand, and lead her in with him: and this glorious bridegroom and bride shall with all their shining ornaments, ascend up together into the heaven of heaven; the whole multitude of glorious angels waiting upon them: and this Son and daughter of God shall, in their united glory and joy, present themselves together before the Father; when Christ shall say 'Here I am, and the children, which thou hast given me': and they both shall in that relation and union, together receive the Father's blessing; and shall thenceforward rejoice together, in consummate, uninterrupted, immutable, and everlasting glory, in the love and embraces of each other, and joint enjoyment of the love of the Father.[7]

You might need to read those words a couple of times to grasp the full power of what Edwards is imagining: the full intimacy, unity, oneness and connectedness with God that will be ours one day very soon. Again, you might like to pray for the help of God's Spirit, the divine intimacy agent, to help you to develop this sort of spiritual imagination. Biblical fuel for it is found most of all in the book of Revelation, which the apostle John wrote while 'in the Spirit' (Revelation 1:10). God's Spirit could be seen as the divine wedding

---

7 Jonathan Edwards in Dane C. Ortlund, *Edwards on the Christian Life: Alive to the Beauty of God* (Wheaton, IL: Crossway, 2014), p. 87.

planner in all the advance details he provides in Revelation 19–22. We should be using them to shape our anticipation of *the* great wedding day. When my sister was struggling to sleep as a child, my mum used to get her to imagine her wedding day. It would do us all good to fall asleep imagining what it will be like when Jesus is finally united with us, his church, forever.

Father, friend and fiancé

As Christian philosopher Dallas Willard puts it, 'God's desire for us is that we should live in him.'[8] Declaring himself to be our Father, friend and fiancé are the three main ways God seeks to help us to begin to grasp this reality with the help of his Holy Spirit. They flesh out what it means for us, in the words of the apostle Peter, to 'participate in the divine nature' (2 Peter 1:4) or, in the words in the prayer of Jesus, to be as much 'in' him and his Father as they are in each other (see, again, John 17:20–21). It should be no surprise that the biblical ways of communicating the most intimate relationship with God possible are the most intimate human relationships we can possibly imagine. We were created to need this divine intimacy most of all. Until we learn to enjoy it more, our lives will be incomplete, so that is where our attention will turn next.

Some of those reading might never have even begun a relationship with God. If that's you, and you want this sort of intimate relationship with the one who created you and loves you in these ways, why not pause and ask him to embrace you right now? Put yourself in the shoes of the prodigal son, repeat his words and relive his experience of receiving the extravagant forgiveness of God.[9] As Augustine of Hippo famously said to God, 'You have made us for yourself, and our heart is restless until it rests in you.'[10] Why not rest in his loving embrace for the very first time today?

---

8 Dallas Willard, *The Divine Conspiracy: Rediscovering Our Hidden Life in God* (London: HarperCollins, 1998), p. 18.
9 If this is you, turn to Luke 15:17–24, use similar words and feel the same divine response.
10 Saint Augustine, *Confessions* (Oxford: Oxford University Press, 1991), p. 3.

2
Enjoying intimacy with God

> The presence of God is the central fact of Christianity. At the heart of the Christian message is God Himself waiting for his redeemed children to push in to conscious awareness of His presence. The type of Christianity that appears now to be in vogue knows this Presence only in theory. It fails to stress the Christian's privilege of present realisation.[1]
> A. W. Tozer

Blockers to intimacy with God

The problem is that all of this talk of intimacy with God and enjoying the presence of God might read well on the page and sound good in theory, but we often fail to enjoy the reality in our daily lives. What's stopping us?

Suffering

For some of us, the very pictures of intimacy that God gives us in Scripture are off-putting. Maybe our biological father so abused us that talk of God as our loving Father in heaven is too hard to compute. Maybe we've never really had intimate friends, so we struggle to grasp how Jesus could be one too. Maybe we've been painfully divorced, so any talk of the joy of an everlasting marriage aggravates a very open wound. It is so important to acknowledge these negative experiences and the impact they might have had on our relationship with God. But, if we are careful, I think that our painful wounds can be the place of greatest emotional connection

---

1 A. W. Tozer, *The Pursuit of God* (New Delhi: OM Publishing, 1987), p. 38.

with the God who wants us to become intimately connected with him.

As a single, same-sex-attracted man, I often used to find weddings to be moments of great pain, advertising a relational intimacy I was seemingly denied. But I now use them as a chance to remind myself of the far greater intimacy we will enjoy with God in Christ when we get married to him. The very moments that used to feel most raw because they are the most intimate – the husband looking down the aisle to his bride, the face-to-face exchange of vows, the first kiss – are just small imitations of a deeper reality that I will get to enjoy.

It's my lack in the here and now that most powerfully makes me feel the connection to the far greater spiritual reality. For others, it's more general suffering that blocks any sense of God's intimate love and care for us. How can he be our loving Father, friend and bridegroom and not heal us from cancer, bring our child to faith or end the loneliness? We are, to be honest, quite angry with him, and that feels reasonable given the yawning gap between his claim to be good and the mess in our lives. We know that loving fathers discipline, friends rebuke and spouses correct, but no one we know would lovingly stand by and let what is happening in our lives continue a second longer.

But though we might desperately want to, now is not the time or place to attempt to solve the problem of evil. As pastor Martyn Lloyd-Jones reminds us, 'God's mind is eternal, and God's ways are so infinitely above us that we must always start by being prepared not to understand immediately anything He does.'[2]

My personal experience is that the very sufferings that no human father, friend or spouse would ever have let me go through (the death of a sister, struggles with my gender and sexuality) are, incredibly, the very experiences that God has most used to help me to know and feel his intimate love for me in Christ. That outcome has not taken away or lessened the continued mourning, crying

---

2 Martyn Lloyd-Jones, *Faith on Trial: Studies in Psalm 73* (Fearn: Christian Heritage, 2008), p. 18.

and pain, but it has, very slowly, helped me to grasp the superiority of the sort of parenting, friendship and marital care he provides. I've kept coming back to these precious words of the puritan minister John Flavel:

> It may support thy heart, to consider that in these troubles God is performing that work in which thy soul would rejoice, if thou didst see the design of it. We are clouded with much ignorance, and are not able to discern how particular providences tend to the fulfilment of God's designs; and therefore, like Israel in the wilderness, are often murmuring, because Providence leads us about in a howling desert, where we are exposed to difficulties; though then he led, and is now leading us, *by the right way to a city of habitations.* If you could but see how God in his secret counsel has exactly laid the whole plan of your salvation, even to the smallest means and circumstances; could you but discern the admirable harmony of divine dispensations, their mutual relations, together with the general respect they all have to the last end; had you the liberty to make your own choice, you would, of all the conditions in the world, choose that in which you now are. Providence is like a curious piece of tapestry made of a thousand shreds, which, single, appear useless, but put together, they represent, a beautiful history to the eye.[3]

These words keep reminding me of the greater power God has, the bigger picture he sees and the deeper and more effective love he has for me. What most confuses me today might soon be the very thing I most praise him for.

Happiness

The perceived opposite of suffering – happiness or contentment – can also get in the way of enjoying intimacy with God. Yes, suffering

---

[3] John Flavel, *Keeping the Heart* (Fearn: Christian Heritage, 1999), p. 40. Emphasis original.

can often lead to bitterness and rejection of God's love, but it can also produce in us a dependence on him that we never experienced when life was going well. I've talked with a couple reeling from the worst of cancer diagnoses, who at the same time were testifying to experiencing a closeness to Jesus that they had never experienced before. This makes complete sense: in human relationships, we're often closest to those we've gone through times of adversity with. Just think of the depth of relationships that veterans share because of what they went through together in wartime.

What can most keep us from enjoying life with God is enjoying life too much without him. When life is going well, when our expectations are being met, when our plans are slotting into place, it can be very easy to feel that we don't need his presence, his help or his love. Writing in a book that tells of his eldest child's profound disabilities, Micheal Beates observes this about the physical geography and linked spiritual history of God's Old Testament people:

> The most fertile quadrant in the north-west part of the land of the Bible – the Jezreel valley and surrounding territory – was the location of the worst apostasy, unfaithfulness, and rejection of God anywhere in the land. Where conditions were most ripe and most hospitable, people tended to forget God, to wander from God, even to outright reject him. But correspondingly, the opposite quadrant – the most arid, dry, hostile, and forsaken part of the land – is where God met people in the quiet desolation of their souls.

This is a strong metaphor for us. When the circumstances of life are comfortable, we are more likely to drift from God. We are in danger of believing that we can be self-sufficient, and faith in God can become merely an intellectual exercise. But when we find ourselves in the desolation of loneliness and pain, doubt and desertion, deprivation and despair, there God meets us – even when we can't hear his voice. This is the way God works.[4]

---

[4] Michael S. Beates, *Disability & The Gospel: How God Uses Our Brokenness to Display His Grace* (Wheaton, IL: Crossway, 2012), p. 51.

The Intimacy Deficit

The greatest barrier to an intimate relationship with God could be a happy life, and the best conditions for it could be real hardship. Certainly, the greatest intimacy with Jesus I've witnessed came out of a life of real suffering, expressed most beautifully by the prayers of a dear friend as she lay dying, in pain, on her hospice bed.

Sin

We might name our sin – our harmful attitudes and actions that damage God, ourselves, others and creation – as the biggest intimacy blocker in our relationship with God. This could come about in at least a couple of ways. Perhaps we're avoiding his company because we know, deep down, of our need to repent of a thought, word or deed (or a whole host of them) but don't really want to. Spending time with Jesus in individual prayer or corporate worship would confront us with the reality of our rejection of him and his ways, so we're trying to avoid his gaze.

No game of hide and seek is more futile than that we attempt to play with God. He is our Father, so he knows where we're most likely to hide. He is our greatest friend, so he will not give up looking for us. He is our lover, so he is longing to be reunited with us. If, as you read these words, you sense that you've been vainly hiding from him, now is the time to set out home, knowing that you'll always be met by his loving embrace.

But you might have confessed your sins and still feel that they are blocking any real intimacy with God. A sense of continued guilt is coming between you and him, especially because you know that you'll soon need to confess that particular sin yet again. Maybe you only ever feel that intimacy has been restored when you've managed to keep a clean sheet for a few days. Maybe a good track record is what makes you feel close to God – any slip-up and you feel the need to slowly earn your way back into his good books.

This is projecting human behaviour onto God. We generally do forgiveness (if we do it) when it has been earned. For us, it's nearly always dependent on lasting change. Most examples of human love wouldn't survive our constant failures to make progress with some of our sins, so we assume that God can't love us anymore either. But the Scriptures tell us that despite our sin, even as we repeatedly sin, before, during and after our sin, God keeps loving us as our divine Father, friend and fiancé, and the biggest offence we can cause him is not to believe in that constant reality.

If you struggle to believe that (I do!), you need to hear these striking words from puritan theologian John Owen: 'The greatest sorrow and burden you can lay on the Father, the greatest unkindness you can do to him is not to believe that he loves you.'[5] Undermining our belief in God's loving care of us has long been the evil one's most effective trick (see his conversation with Eve in Genesis 3). We need to call him out on it. Everything God has said and done, everything he ever asks of us, rises out of his love for us, and that love will *never* give up on us. It is, in some memorable words from my favourite children's Bible, 'A Never Stopping, Never Giving Up, Unbreaking, Always and Forever Love'.[6]

Catalysts for intimacy with God

How do you counter these powerful intimacy blockers? How do you develop a close, intimate, lasting connection with God even in the middle of suffering, or happiness, or sin, or whatever you're going through right now? We could go in any number of directions at this point: things we can do together or alone, spiritual practices from church history or different parts of the world. But this is just an introduction to intimacy with God, so I'm going to focus on one thing we can all do – whoever we are, wherever we are and whatever company we might be enjoying right now. It's a universal solution to any lack of felt intimacy with God.

Adopt a psalm

I think that the most helpful first step in growing our sense of connectedness to him can be this simple: we open our Bibles and turn to the greatest expressions of lived intimacy with God, which are

---

[5] John Owen, abridged by R. J. K. Law, *Communion with God* (Edinburgh: Banner of Truth, 1991), p. 17.
[6] Sally Lloyd Jones, *The Jesus Storybook Bible* (Grand Rapids, MI: Zonderkidz, 2007), p. 36.

the Psalms, the beautifully preserved prayer book of God's ancient people. As pastor Eugene Peterson puts it:

> There is no literature in all the world that is more true to life and more honest than Psalms, for here we have warts-and-all religion. Every skeptical thought, every disappointing venture, every pain, every despair that we can face is lived through and integrated into a personal, saving relationship with God – a relationship that also has in it acts of praise, blessing, peace, security, trust, and love.[7]

In reading the varied words the psalmists have left, we get to learn what it's like to stay connected and to feel united with God in all circumstances, through all emotions, and in all personality types.

As a child, I was taught how to draw by tracing images drawn by much more experienced artists than me. I learned shapes and perspective from following the lines they had drawn before. As children of God, we're taught how to enjoy intimacy with God by those who have enjoyed it before us. We can learn the shape of it and the perspective you need for it by following the lines they have written before.

The good news is that whoever you are and whatever your personality, feelings and circumstances, there will be a psalm – or part of one – written by someone similar who has been there too. God has preserved their words to be a catalyst for intimacy in your relationship with him. The practical challenge is to find the right psalm and then to adopt it, to make its words, its pictures and its feelings your own in prayer and praise and in lament and longing.

So, for example, if your levels of happiness and trust in God are riding high, Psalm 103 will help you to communicate that. If, like me so often, you're cynical about God and his promises, you could adopt Psalm 73. If you're constantly being wowed by the beauty of creation, you could use Psalm 19:1–6. If you're drowning in guilt,

---

[7] Eugene H. Peterson, *A Long Obedience in the Same Direction: Discipleship in an Instant Society* (San Francisco, CA: IVP USA, 2000), p. 69.

you could benefit from spending a lot of time with Psalm 51. If you're grateful for your lot in life, why not learn and use Psalm 16? If you're very angry with God right now, he has kindly given you the words to use in Psalm 88. In the light of that last example, theologian Belden Lane is right in saying:

> The Psalmist insists that if the only prayer we have to offer is one of bitter anguish, we pray it nonetheless. The poet knows that in the release of anger, intimacy is realized. God longs for whatever lies in the depths of the soul.[8]

There is a danger that we think that the psalms written out of anger or disappointment are less spiritually beneficial than those that express praise or trust. But expressing *all* of our emotions can build a more intimate, connected relationship with God. The words and emotions of Psalm 88, expressing feelings of disconnection from God, self, others and creation, are still cried out to him in the expectation that he is listening. Whatever we are feeling, the key thing is to talk to him in the light of who he is and what he does. The Psalms train us to do that in each and every circumstance of life.

To discover which psalm you would do well to adopt right now, you could ask an older Christian you trust about which might best fit you and your circumstances. They will be especially helpful if their personality and history are similar to yours, or you could just read through them all until you find one you feel a connection with.

Try a psalm on for size and find another one if it's too big or too small. Wear it for as long as it feels comfortable for you, and aim to change the psalm you adopt regularly. Different seasons of life will fit best with different psalms. Perhaps ask your pastor to prescribe one for you – there are dangers in constant self-medication. Remember that it might just be part of a psalm that most helps

---

8 Belden C. Lane, *Ravished by Beauty: The Surprising Legacy of Reformed Spirituality* (Oxford: Oxford University Press, 2011), p. 95.

you connect with God – don't feel you have to adopt the whole of Psalm 119! It might even be just a phrase or verse. I was kept going through a Covid lockdown in 2020 by half a verse from Psalm 31: 'My times are in your hands' (Psalm 31:15). These are such reassuring and intimate words.

Adopt Psalm 23

If you struggle to find the right fit, the good news is that there are some multi-purpose psalms that have helped numerous people in different times and circumstances to connect with God. They tend to be the most popular ones, and the most popular of all is Psalm 23. For the rest of this chapter, I'm going to show how I've used it as a catalyst for intimacy with God in my life, encouraged by Jesus, who would have prayed this psalm himself. It fits him best, and it helps us to recognise him as the good shepherd it describes:

> I am the good shepherd; I know my sheep and my sheep know me – just as the Father knows me and I know the Father – and I lay down my life for the sheep.
> (John 10:14–15)

This close relationship between a shepherd and his sheep is yet another biblical picture of the intimate relationship God enjoys with us in the Old and New Testaments. It was, of course, an obvious relationship for the original shepherd king, David, to draw upon as he reflected on how the Creator God of the universe cared for him:

> The LORD is my shepherd, I lack nothing.
>   He makes me lie down in green pastures,
> he leads me beside quiet waters,
>   he refreshes my soul.
> He guides me along the right paths
>   for his name's sake.
> Even though I walk
>   through the darkest valley,

I will fear no evil,
    for you are with me;
your rod and your staff,
    they comfort me.

You prepare a table before me
    in the presence of my enemies.
You anoint my head with oil;
    my cup overflows.
Surely your goodness and love will follow me
    all the days of my life,
and I will dwell in the house of the LORD
    forever.
(Psalm 23:1–6)

I've recently spent as much time in this psalm as possible, seeking to enjoy, feel, experience and know the intimacy it describes. To achieve that, I've done a whole host of different things:

- I've *said it* out loud, putting the stress on different words: 'The Lord *is* my shepherd', then 'The Lord is *my* shepherd.' Just going through the alternative ways of reading each verse can get you thinking about what is being said in deeper ways and making new connections.
- I've *read it* in a range of translations, being especially helped by those that communicate old truths in new ways. I love Eugene Peterson's version of the beginning of verse 5: 'You serve me a six-course dinner' (Psalm 23:5, MSG). God is a generous host.
- I've *studied it* to learn from the insights of those who understand the original Hebrew, scholars and pastors who can stop me from misunderstanding and misapplying it. So often, small details – like the original sense of God's goodness and love pursuing us – have had a massive impact on me.[9]

---

[9] My top recommendation would be David Gibson, *The Lord of Psalm 23: Jesus Our Shepherd, Companion, and Host* (Wheaton, IL: Crossway, 2023).

The Intimacy Deficit

- I've *learned it*, so I can ponder it when walking in the park, queuing at the supermarket or lying sleepless in bed at night. Instant recall of its words, as well as moments of struggling to remember which exact word comes next, have helped me to speak its truths into my daily life.
- I've *heard it* sung in different settings by musicians who do imaginative things. One contemporary setting[10] repeats talk of God's goodness and mercy following us at greater and greater speed, so it begins to feel like I'm being pursued by them – which, of course, I am.
- I've *sung it* – individually and corporately – in different versions that have helped me to see and feel how it applies in different ways.[11] It turns out that it can provide comfort and challenge at both a wedding and a funeral – sometimes in the very same setting of the words and music.
- I've *prayed it* at different times, allowing it to shape what I'm saying to God for myself and for others. Using it to set the agenda of my prayers has got me praying for much deeper, more consequential things than I would instinctively pray for on my own.
- I've *applied it* with precision in my life. When, for instance, I think that I need a new stylish flat on Bristol's Harbourside to be happy in life, I've used the opening sentence to remind myself that I already have everything I need.
- I've *shared it* with others in daily conversation, praying it into their lives and applying it to the circumstances they are facing. Sometimes, this has been a direct quote. At other times, it's just an allusion that connects both me and them to our Shepherd's powerful presence and care.
- I've *painted it*. A church staff fun day saw us decorating mugs, and I enjoyed painting a series of images to encapsulate the message of the psalm. Picking the images that connected with

---

10 William Todd's 'The Lord is my Shepherd'.
11 My current favourite is City Alight's 'Shepherd'. See https://cityalight.com/song/shepherd/.

me was a deeply personal experience. I love drinking from that mug!
- I've *imagined it*, developing the imagery of the psalm in my mind's eye: the spread that God has laid out for me, the thought of him serving *me*. George Herbert's famous poem 'Love III' has encouraged and shaped this powerful experience.
- I've *experienced it* as I've consumed bread and wine with others during the Lord's Supper. The communion table is one that he has prepared with physical food and drink to sustain us spiritually in the middle of the battle that life so often is.
- I've *watched it* acted out in life as a shepherd gathered his flock together in the English Lake District, and as a friend went to so much self-sacrificial effort to host a dinner party where everyone was well provided for, and no one felt left out of things.
- I've *updated it* myself, trying to think of how the agricultural imagery of the opening verses might translate into my contemporary urban context. A doctor who works among my city's homeless re-expressed the opening words as 'The Lord is my caseworker.'

My hope is that the above list includes something that helps you to connect this psalm, or another, with your life – or sparks better ideas. Our contrasting personalities and circumstances will mean that different things appeal or work. Regardless, the aim is to allow the intimacy with God that David is describing, that Jesus experienced, to draw you into a similarly close, connected relationship with God in Christ. It has for me.

Encouragement to intimacy with God

All of this might sound a little bit too much like hard work, but taking and using the Psalms to better enjoy intimacy with God is much easier than the alternative: constructing our own words and ways of doing that. So many of us struggle to make our times of Bible reading and prayer feel like genuine communion or connection with God, and I think that is because we separate them too much in our minds. One of the best things about the Psalms is that they are both God's word to us *and* they give us the words to speak to him. In one of his helpful books on the Psalms, Eugene Peterson makes this point about them:

> Scripture and prayer are not two separate entities. My pastoral work was to fuse them into a single act: scriptureprayer or prayerscripture. It is this fusion of God speaking to us (Scripture) and us speaking to him (prayer) that the Holy Spirit uses to form the life of Christ in us.[12]

That is what I've discovered having adopted Psalm 23. As I recite it in my head, to my heart, I'm both hearing God speak to me *and* speaking to him at the very same time. The opening words, 'The Lord is my shepherd,' are words of comfort from him and a chance for me to declare my faith in him. Whether 'scriptureprayer' or 'prayerscripture', both are enabling precious intimacy with God.

This intimacy is the best thing about being a Christian: not Jesus' incarnation, crucifixion, or resurrection (as amazing as they are), but what they achieve for you and me – the closest of relationships with the Creator God of the universe as our loving parent, constant companion and devoted spouse. This is a present reality that we will only fully enjoy in his new creation, but even now we can experience so much more intimacy with him by encountering him through the Psalms. The next time you feel an intimacy deficit, some of the best places you can go are these poems written by people like us, for people like us, to enjoy the God who knows and loves us best.

In any given day, we all take much-needed breaks. However, modern life means that we often feel compelled to fill those little pauses by swiping through social media, or perhaps even dating apps or porn. We're looking for something or someone to connect with, even to complete us. We've been tricked into thinking that a

---

12 Peterson, *A Long Obedience in the Same Direction*, p. 196.

new look, laugh, house, person or experience will meet our needs, but only an intimate relationship with our Creator will truly satisfy us. We were created for nothing less. Start swiping through the Psalms until you find the one that most connects you to him. Use it to take your daily breaks in the company of your Father, friend and fiancé. He is longing to enjoy your company through them.

Intimacy with God: questions for reflection and discussion

- What is intimacy with God?
- Which biblical picture most helps you to appreciate it?
- What stops you from enjoying intimacy with God?
- Which psalm might help you to enjoy it more?
- How could you best enjoy that psalm?

Further reading

Tim Chester, *Enjoying God: Experience the Power and Love of God in Everyday Life* (Epsom: The Good Book Company, 2018).

3
Intimacy with yourself

> Intimacy requires a solid sense of self to be successful and satisfying.[1]
> *Olivia Laing*

Delighting in yourself

Talk of intimacy with yourself can sound slightly odd, even inappropriate. What exactly are we exploring here?! It's something like this: us being at ease with ourselves, content as the woman or man God has made us to be, delighting in the body, the personality, the strengths and weaknesses that he has made us with. It's knowing yourself, having writer Olivia Laing's 'solid sense of self' as a firm foundation for other relationships. It's about being positively connected, at one and at peace with who we have been created to be rather than wanting to be someone else. It's being able to join David in saying these sorts of words with integrity:

> For you created my inmost being;
>   you knit me together in my mother's womb.
> I praise you because I am fearfully and wonderfully made;
>   your works are wonderful,
>   I know that full well.
> My frame was not hidden from you
>   when I was made in the secret place,
>   when I was woven together in the depths of the earth.

---

1 Olivia Laing, *The Lonely City* (Edinburgh: Canongate, 2017), p. 241.

Intimacy with yourself

Your eyes saw my unformed body;
  all the days ordained for me were written in your book
  before one of them came to be.
How precious to me are your thoughts, God!
  How vast is the sum of them!
Were I to count them,
  they would outnumber the grains of sand –
  when I awake, I am still with you.
(Psalm 139:13–18)

King David is marvelling at himself and praising God as a result. He could have been reflecting on the incredible complexity of the bones and muscles in his hand. He might have been looking back at the range of feelings, the highs and lows, that he was capable of on any given day. He could have been thinking about his capacity to create and rule as a divine image-bearer. Regardless, he can delight in the person who God has created him to be, in his uniqueness, and in God's care for every part of him every day of his life.

We should be working and praying for a similar gratitude to God for who he has made us to be in all of our physical, emotional, skilful complexity and diversity. Intimacy with ourselves is about getting to this point: when everything God has made us to be, in all its beautiful messiness, makes us gasp with delight and fuels our praise of him.

How near to that point are you? Most of us are miles away. We cannot make King David's words our own and, if we're being honest, we think that the expectation that we might is a little bit laughable. Yes, if we had a body like Michaelangelo's *David* (or the female equivalent), then we might praise God for it, but that's not what we avoided looking at in the mirror this morning. If we produced the sort of beautiful lyrics David seemingly churned out on a daily basis, then we might make some of those words about God's goodness to us, but we can't write like him. If we spent our days ruling a prosperous and growing kingdom that God had gifted us, then we might delight in ourselves a bit more, but our current job seems to be as high as we can expect to go. King David's realities are not our realities: we're jealous of other people's bodies, skills and positions – especially ones like his.

Except that the New Testament would contend that we have more reason to feel good about ourselves, to delight in ourselves, than King David (I will attempt to persuade you of this in a moment). His words in Psalm 139 could and should be words we can say with even more enthusiasm than him. How can we possibly begin to make them our own?

Delighting in *whose* you are

We need to start by building solid and lasting foundations, asking what can be true of all of us, all the time, if we're Christians. This foundation is a delight in ourselves whatever our personality type, background or people skills, a delight in ourselves that can survive our bodies ageing, our mental faculties fading or our careers ending. This will be the focus of this chapter, before the next chapter explores the more temporary delight we might take in our physical capacities, our emotional intelligence or our work achievements. I think that cultural commentator David Brooks gives us a push in the right direction by pointing out, 'The crucial question is not, Who am I? but, Whose am I?'[2] The Bible's answers to that key question can help us to begin to delight in ourselves, in all the ways and circumstances that God wants us to, without disappearing into either unhealthy introspection (because the biblical answers come from outside of ourselves), or sinful idolatry (because the biblical answers should fuel our worship of God).

We are God's creatures

God made you and me. As King David memorably puts it, 'You knit me together in my mother's womb' (Psalm 139:13). He made us to belong to him, to be his dependent children, his image-bearers. Some of the most value-giving words ever spoken are these:

---

2 David Brooks, *The Second Mountain: The Quest for a Moral Life* (London: Allen Lane, 2019), p. 310.

Intimacy with yourself

> So God created mankind in his own image,
>   in the image of God he created them;
>   male and female he created them.
> (Genesis 1:27)

So much flows from these words (they are, for instance, the root of all talk of human rights), but I love how pastor Steve DeWitt helps us to *feel* the personal impact of them:

> The wonderland of God's creation includes a masterpiece whose beauty more closely resembles the actual nature of God than anything else in the whole universe. What is it? You.[3]

I recently met the daughter of a distant cousin for the first time. There was no need for her to introduce herself because she was the spitting image of her mum – I didn't have to be told whose family she belonged to! We are, in many ways, so much like our Creator that our parentage is not in doubt. In everything we have the capacity to think, do and say, it's abundantly clear that we belong to him.

All of this gives me a value that I need to begin to grasp as I look in the mirror in the morning. I see the weary look of a middle-aged man in a body I've often struggled to love, but God says that I see someone who is like him, who belongs to him, who was created to depend on him, who has been made to represent him to the world around me and whom he has always loved. I should be delighting in *whose* I am in him before anything else. It will give me a dignity to delight in until my dying day.

We are ruins restored

But what about the damage that our sin, our rejection of God, has done to us? Surely the events of Genesis 3, repeated in each of our lives, cancel all the positives in what I've been saying and

---
3 Steve DeWitt, *Eyes Wide Open: Enjoying God in Everything* (Grand Rapids, MI: Credo House, 2012), p. 73.

ruin everything? How can we take delight in being the sinners, the rebels against God, we have become?

Some of us do need to be reminded of our sin and the damage it has done to our relationship with God, ourselves, others and creation. We too instinctively turn a blind eye to it. Perhaps we come from a church background where its all-pervasive reality was played down to make the gospel more acceptable, or we were shaped by a culture where any such negative talk was seen as harmful. But my guess is that many of us allow our sin to define us too often, to shape our view of ourselves too much, in ways that stop us from properly delighting in whose we have become.

In contrast, the apostle Paul, writing to the Ephesian Christians, is very clear on the radical break that has been made with our sinful past and our new status if we turn to Jesus in repentance and faith:

> As for you, you were dead in your transgressions and sins, in which you used to live when you followed the ways of this world and of the ruler of the kingdom of the air, the spirit who is now at work in those who are disobedient. All of us also lived among them at one time, gratifying the cravings of our flesh and following its desires and thoughts. Like the rest, we were by nature deserving of wrath. But because of his great love for us, God, who is rich in mercy, made us alive with Christ even when we were dead in transgressions – it is by grace you have been saved.
> (Ephesians 2:1–5)

We were once dead to God because of our sin. We belonged not to him but to his great opponent, the devil. We lived for ourselves, having cruelly rejected him who has generously given us absolutely everything, making us more than deserving of his right anger or 'wrath'. But now, purely down to God's loving kindness and grace, we've been spiritually resurrected, given new life through Jesus' death and resurrection. We now belong to him doubly through his creation *and* redemption of us. We were once ruins, but now we've been restored by a new owner.

Intimacy with yourself

We often fail to really get how great the change has been. Bible teacher John Stott seeks to help us with typical clarity:

> Our biography is written in two volumes. Volume one is the story of the old man, the old self, of me before my conversion. Volume two is the story of the new man, the new self, of me after I was made a new creation in Christ. Volume one of my biography ended with the judicial death of the old self. I was a sinner. I deserved to die. I did die. I received my deserts in my Substitute with whom I have become one. Volume two of my biography opened with my resurrection. My old life having finished, a new life to God has begun.[4]

We need to embrace our new life, our new status. We are no longer biblically defined as sinners but as saints, fully restored to a relationship with God. That is how he now sees us and treats us. We need to learn to delight in ourselves because of everything that is now true of us due to our union with Christ.

We are united to Christ

Our union with Jesus is one of the most repeated ideas in the New Testament. It's at the heart of the intimacy we enjoy with him, so great that we are now talked of as having become one with him, united with him forever. What he has been through in the past, we've been through too because we are spiritually connected to him. The close relationship he enjoys with God in the present is open to us to enjoy because we now share his status as God's Son.

The apostle Paul is constantly rejoicing in this reality, most powerfully of all in Galatians:

> I have been crucified with Christ and I no longer live, but Christ lives in me. The life I now live in the body, I live by faith in the Son of God, who loved me and gave himself for me. (Galatians 2:20)

---

4 John R. W Stott in Philip Graham Ryken, *The Message of Salvation* (London: IVP UK, 2001), p. 242.

Do you get what Paul is saying about himself? What we get to say about ourselves too? My whole history and identity, my whole past and present, are now bound up in Christ's history and identity, his past death for me. The new status I enjoy in the here and now is because I'm joined, by faith, to him who lost his life for me.

I love how the great communicator C. S. Lewis grounds all of this theology, which is often hard to get our hearts and minds around, in the simple act of us praying the Lord's Prayer:

> Its very first words are *Our Father*. Do you now see what those words mean? They mean quite frankly, that you are putting yourself in the place of the Son of God. To put it bluntly, you are *dressing up as Christ*.[5]

How do I dare to act as if I were Jesus? Because Jesus has dressed himself up as me! Because he has taken away my sin and faced my spiritual death, I now have the full access to God that he enjoys, united to him, dressed as the spotless, sinless Son of God.

That is something I can unambiguously delight in. I don't know if you've ever got a new outfit that made you look so good and feel so good that it changed the way you thought of yourself or how other people treated you for a while – perhaps your very first suit, a military uniform or your wedding dress. We get to enjoy that sort of new outfit now we are united with Christ, except the change in our feelings and status it brings is permanent: we will delight in our new look forever. Even when the best of outfits fail to make us look good to others, we'll always look good to God – dressed like Jesus and united with Christ.

A hesitancy that some people express about this talk of all Christians being united to Christ is the worry that it destroys our individuality and our sense of self by merging us completely with him and with each other. This is an obvious contemporary Western concern where the individual rules supreme, but the New Testament, while stressing the communal, does not erase the

---

5 C. S. Lewis, *Mere Christianity* (Glasgow: William Collins, 2012), p. 187. Emphasis original.

individual. It makes very clear that union with Christ does not undermine our uniqueness.

The body analogy, which Paul famously employs in 1 Corinthians, is very helpful in communicating this: 'Just as a body, though one, has many parts, but all its many parts form one body, so it is with Christ' (1 Corinthians 12:12). As Christ's body, we – the church, Christians – are part of him, that close and connected to him. But we are all different body parts. We make up the same body, but we all play different roles determined by the different circumstances, personalities and gifts God has given us. Some of these are listed by Paul in the verses before. The majority are not, but the point is clear: there is real diversity in Christ's body alongside a unity of identity and purpose. I love how pastor Rankin Wilbourne communicates this:

> Our self is not obliterated by our union with Christ; our self is fully realized. God the Creator clearly delights in our unique particularity. From sunsets to snowflakes, he makes endless variations of beautiful things for the sheer joy of it. He never repeats himself and never runs out of ideas.[6]

We can and should delight in being utterly unique. Yes, we have a shared genetic inheritance with our biological family members, and we have a shared spiritual identity with our church family members. But we can also, as individuals, say with David that, '*I am fearfully and wonderfully made*.' In creating you with a particular physical body, in gifting you with a distinct personality, in restoring you through your union with Christ, God was creating a one-off masterpiece and, like all great artists, he wants his work to be appreciated – most especially by you.

We are gifted by God's Spirit

Our individuality is underlined by Paul's insistence that we each have a unique but equally valuable role to play, which is determined

---

6 Rankin Wilbourne, *Union with Christ: The Way to Know and Enjoy God* (Colorado Springs, CO: David Cook, 2016), p. 162.

by the different ways God's Spirit has gifted us. Your unique gifts make you indispensable to the rest of the body. Famously, 'The eye cannot say to the hand, "I don't need you!" And the head cannot say to the feet, "I don't need you!"' (1 Corinthians 12:21). We all need each other in our gifted differences. God has gifted each of us in different ways. Our challenge is to find our individual gifts and use them to build up the whole body, the corporate whole.

So, what gifts has God's Spirit given you? Some will be him taking your unique personality, pre-existing abilities and natural strengths and using them to glorify God. Perhaps you've always been an instinctive leader, or very good with figures, and that's why God's Spirit has got you leading that team or working as an accountant. Some gifts are more supernatural. Perhaps God's Spirit seemed to zap you with them when you became a Christian or when your church needed them for a particular season. Perhaps previously, it might have been fair to say that you were not famous for your wisdom and discernment, but that is now what people most appreciate about you – your small group and the wider church instinctively turn to you when it comes to applying God's word to our lives today, and you have the spiritual gift of 'guidance' (see 1 Corinthians 12:28).

Some gifts come and go. They might determine how we serve for decades, and then new circumstances, like a change in our health, mean that we can no longer use them. God gives us new gifts, new ways of serving him. So many senior saints I know have been given the gifts of prayer or encouragement in their final years when other contexts for service are no longer physically possible for them.

Whoever you are, at whatever season of life, if you're a Christian, then God's Spirit has uniquely gifted you to keep serving his body, the church. He has left no one out: 'Now to each one the manifestation of the Spirit is given for the common good' (1 Corinthians 12:7).

'Each one' of us has received gifts from God's Spirit. You should always be actively finding out what gifts he has given you (by trying new things out and getting good feedback) so you can use your unique mix of gifts for the good of others and delight in being

God's gift to the wider whole: a body that would be at a loss without your unique contribution.

Returning to King David

You have been created by God, and although ruined by sin, have been restored and united to Christ and gifted by God's Spirit. This puts you in a far better position than King David was the first time he felt and wrote verses 13–18 of Psalm 139. His words are true of us too, but we could add to them in the light of the extra riches that are ours through the cross of Christ and the sending of his Spirit. King David could not delight in the death of God for him and the permanent residence of the Spirit of God within him (the Holy Spirit seems to come and go from God's Old Testament people), but we – incredibly – can. Rather than being jealous of him for his good looks, poetic skills and regal status, we should be open to the possibility that he would be jealous of us and would swap them all for what we now get to enjoy in Jesus.

Just one way of appreciating our better position in the here and now would be to prayerfully personalise the summary of spiritual blessings the apostle Paul opens his letter to the Ephesian Christians with. Yes, these are true of all of them together, but he also wanted them to feel the reality of them individually too:

> Praise be to the God and Father of our Lord Jesus Christ, who has blessed us [*me*] in the heavenly realms with every spiritual blessing in Christ. For he chose us [*me*] in him before the creation of the world to be holy and blameless in his sight. In love he predestined us [*me*] for adoption to sonship through Jesus Christ, in accordance with his pleasure and will – to the praise of his glorious grace, which he has freely given us [*me*] in the One he loves. In him we [*I*] have redemption through his blood, the forgiveness of sins, in accordance with the riches of God's grace that he lavished on us [*me*]. With all wisdom and understanding, he made known to us [*me*] the mystery of his will according to his good pleasure, which he

purposed in Christ, to be put into effect when the times reach their fulfilment – to bring unity to all things in heaven and on earth under Christ.
(Ephesians 1:3–10)

May praying those words spark our delight in *whose* we are today. They certainly provide a solid sense of self, which can provide feelings of success and satisfaction whatever might happen to us. We have in him both an inheritance and a linked identity that will never perish, spoil or fade.

4
Enjoying intimacy with yourself

> A Ford car trying to be a Cadillac is absurd, but if a Ford accepts itself as a Ford, it can do many things that a Cadillac could never do: it can get in parking spaces that a Cadillac can never get in. And in life some of us are Fords and some of us are Cadillacs.[1]
> *Martin Luther King Jr*

Blockers to intimacy with yourself

The last chapter saw us talking about what is true of all Christians: we are created by God, ruined by sin, restored by our union with Christ and gifted by God's Spirit. This chapter is going to see us seek to spend our time delighting in what is true of us as individual, uniquely formed Christians: enjoying who our personal genetics, histories, personalities, strengths and weaknesses have made us to be. Intimacy with ourselves is not just about connecting with *whose* we are, but *who* he has made us to be. As we seek to do that, we'll start by naming the things that often block us from making these life-giving connections.

False promises

The motivational poster boldly declares, 'You can be whoever you want to be!' but that, we discover, is simply not true. As Martin Luther King points out, some are rarely noticed Fords, others are head-turning Cadillacs, and we need to recognise the limitations

---

1 Martin Luther King Jr, 'The Three Dimensions of a Complete Life' in *Letter from a Birmingham Jail* (London: Penguin Modern, 2018), p. 34.

(and advantages) of what we've been made to be. Let me list just some of the things that I can never be with the body God has given me: a tennis player (my eyesight means that I can't see the ball), a woman (my DNA is a man's), or a man with one of those perfectly toned torsos (I don't have that sort of body and/or self-discipline). Although I have, at different stages of my life, dreamed of being each of these things, they are just not possible for someone like me.

One of the most life-giving things any of us can learn is that we cannot be whoever we want to be. God has not made me to be any of those things – and that is OK. The God who knit me together in my mother's womb has stitched into my life male chromosomes, a lack of binocular vision and an unimpressive torso. I can only be what *he* wants me to be. He has his plans and purposes in all things, and it's best for me to learn to accept that – even in the areas I find hardest.

Rather than believing in our culture's false promises, our lives would be better if we learned to live happily with who we are or what it is realistically possible for us to become. That won't be an easy journey. A friend of mine has spent decades reciting Psalm 139:13–18 into the mirror, but that has still been a more effective treatment than the surgery that would never really have made her who she wanted to be. Better the painful realities of who God has made us to be than the world's false promises of who we will never be.[2]

False humility

Secular lies need to be done away with if we're to enjoy intimacy with ourselves, but Christian lies need to be repented of too. It would be lovely to say that it's only our non-Christian culture that stops us from being at ease with ourselves, but it's also the church. Too many Christians I meet think that being godly means having a very low view of yourself and your gifts – or even denying their very existence. I can't tell you how many times a sister or brother in

---

2 For further help with some of the painful experiences we touch on here, see the relevant resources at https:/www.livingout.org and Preston Sprinkle, *Embodied: Transgender, the Church & What the Bible Has to Say* (Colorado Springs, CO: David Cook, 2021).

Christ has failed to take a compliment or encouragement. I've said something like, 'You led those prayers beautifully!' and that truth has been immediately, instinctively denied. Sometimes, the reason will be a paralysing under-confidence but often, I fear, it comes from a false humility – a low estimation of ourselves and our gifts that many seem to equate with being a good Christian. We think that it's wrong to think or say or hear that we're good at something.

This might just be a British Christian problem (we're infamous for our self-deprecation), but American professor Karen Swallow Prior applies a story about the Christian novelist Flannery O'Connor in a way that implies that it might be a more universal problem:

> Once, when asked by a student at a lecture, 'Miss O'Connor, why do you write?' she answered, 'Because I am good at it.' At first glance, this reply might seem conceited or proud. But the truth is that knowing what we are good at and what we are not, doing what we are supposed to do, and not what we aren't, being what we are supposed to be and not what we aren't, is the essence of true humility.[3]

There is a woman at ease with herself, enjoying intimacy with herself and the person who God has made her to be!

Catalysts for intimacy with yourself

How can we follow Miss O'Connor's good – and I think godly – example? We can join her in the following actions.

Speaking the truth about ourselves

If we are good at something, we should say so. If we aren't good at something, we should say so. If we aren't sure whether we are good

---

3 Karen Swallow Prior, *On Reading Well: Finding the Good Life Through Great Books* (Ada, MI: Brazos, 2018), p. 236.

at it or not, we should say so. We should practise Christian ethics 101: we should tell the truth.

Imagine yourself in a planning meeting for some Christian event, Sunday service or church building project (we're focusing on Christian contexts because we're especially bad at this). A relatively skilled task needs to be completed, and you know that you have the necessary personality, gifts and capacity, so why not say so? 'I'm good at that! I'll do it.' Admit to being the person who God has created you to be and gifted you to be. Don't stare at the floor, but catch the chairperson's eye and volunteer.

Later in the meeting, the person in the chair is trying to catch your eye because you've already volunteered for something, and they now see you as a soft target. But this time, it's something you've done before and it was a disaster – you don't have the right personality or the real skill it takes. Feel free to say so! The words 'I'm not the right person for that job!' demonstrate self-awareness and an intimate knowledge of yourself, which is speaking the truth for the good of everyone in the room and everything you're trying to do together.

Picking up on the imagery of 1 Corinthians 12, we should be developing our sense of what body part God has made us to be and communicating that reality to others. Yes, there are tasks that all body parts should be doing (like praying for unbelievers and welcoming strangers), and there is a danger of being too picky when some jobs just need to be done by someone (like pouring the coffee or rearranging the chairs), but God has given you a unique role too. If we are a foot and people are trying to get us to function as a hand, then that will be uncomfortable for us and potentially steal the role God has equipped someone else in our church family to fill. Too many churches are full of body parts in the wrong places because people have not been very good at speaking the truth about themselves, at saying 'no' to doing something God has not created them to do.

Personally, it has taken me ages to say the words 'I chair meetings well!' I even came out about my sexuality before I could come out about this. You might think that this is because it's not really the most impressive superpower or personality trait, that there are more exciting gifts and people – and you're right. But if you've sat through as many badly chaired meetings as I have (in numerous different contexts), the gift of chairing them well – planning and completing a realistic agenda, having and hearing all the right voices, keeping each item to time and keeping the discussions focused – is rare, and too many people who shouldn't be doing it are struggling on without the necessary skills. If only those who have them would be brave enough to volunteer, and those who don't would be honest enough to step down!

How is this brave new world going to come about? By all of us listening to feedback from others.

Listening to feedback

I learned that I was good at chairing meetings by other people saying so, by their appreciative comments as we ended on time with decisions made and people feeling heard.[4] Discerning gifts is a community project, and we need to become better at giving each other the information we need to work out who God has made us to be.

At my church, when an elder or staff member steps down, we've developed the habit of going around the table at their last meeting and each sharing something we're going to especially miss about them. By the end of this exercise, we've in effect carried out a 'personality and giftings audit' on them, and I know that each of them has left massively encouraged. But on one level, the conversation comes too late, bringing clarity about how God has made and gifted them as they're walking out of the door (though we pray that their gifts will be used in new contexts).

I would love for us all to become much better at giving, inviting and receiving feedback as a natural part of church family life together. I want to see people get to know themselves – and their God-given strengths and weaknesses – because other people have

---

4 My apologies if you have been part of one of those meetings that I've failed to chair as well as I might and are finding all of this hard to take. Further apologies if this is the sort of self-deprecating comment that shows that I'm too English and struggling to apply my own advice.

got to know them and shared that information. Some of us are too under-confident to ever notice our gifts. Others need their sense of giftedness in something to be corrected. We *all* need the outside perspective of other people to rightly assess our inside perspective of the person God has made us to be.

Of course, not all feedback is equal. Some of it comes from those who know us well and some from those who don't know the full story. Some comes from people with real spiritual insight and some from the well-meaning who just want to say something nice. One of the challenges of working out our gifts is finding the people whom God has gifted at helping people to discover their own gifts.

Weirdly, one of the most helpful ways for me was reading my old school reports. When my parents downsized, a whole dusty file of them was enthusiastically passed on to me. Reading what was being said about my strengths and weaknesses from ages eight to eighteen, it was unnerving to see how little I've changed, how the same feedback is still being given in appraisals at work today.[5] This could have depressed me, but I found it affirming to read how God has given me such consistent input on who he has, and hasn't, created me to be.

If you don't have similar clarity from the past, ask those you know best today for some feedback and carefully listen to what they say. Try not to be defensive when they say things you find hard – instead, openly welcome everything they say about you, especially what might contradict your opinion of yourself. Be aware that many of your weaknesses will be the shadow-side of your strengths. It can be confusing to have people in one context compliment you for something people in another context have criticised you for.

Could your small group help by dedicating an evening or two to going around the group and appreciating one another in turn? 'What I love about you is...' We once did this, and it was both excruciating (for the English group members) and encouraging (for all). Too many Christians go for far too long without knowing

---

[5] The accuracy of my school reports is probably helped by the unusual fact that I lived at nearly all of my schools either as the child of teachers or as a boarder. The staff writing them knew me well.

how much their sisters and brothers in Christ value their personality or skills. We've yet to find the courage to go around the group and say, 'What I find hard about you is...' but I've found that my small group members are generally more aware of their weaknesses than their strengths, so it feels as if that's less of a pressing need.

Why not sign up for a short-term mission trip, a church holiday club or a summer camp where you'll be thrown in at the deep end and quickly discover what gifts you have and haven't got? I learned so much about myself serving on an annual summer holiday for teenagers in my twenties and thirties. I tried new things and got positive and negative feedback from people who saw me in action.

You could also begin to take the initiative in telling people what you most appreciate about their personalities and the gifts you see them using to build up the church or steward God's world. I'm trying to do this, taking any opportunity to highlight what I find most encouraging about others and what they uniquely contribute to the body and world we are part of.

Noting your main passions

Another thing that can be helpful, by yourself and in conversation with others, is simply clocking the things that most engage or energise you. Experienced pastors Tim Lane and Paul David Tripp are helpful on this:

> One good way to determine your gifts is to ask yourself where you see weaknesses in the body. It is highly likely that you see these weaknesses because you are looking at the church through the lens of your gifts. Where you see weakness is probably the very place where God wants you to serve your brothers and sisters.[6]

I've seen the truth in these words time and time again. The people who have shared their frustration about the lack of something in

---

[6] Timothy S. Lane and Paul David Tripp, *How People Change* (Greensboro, NC: New Growth Press, 2007), p. 89.

the life of our church body are the very body parts God has provided to meet the need. In my life, the weaknesses I've most seen in the churches I've been part of have been exactly the contexts where God has used my personality and gifts most.

Recently, I've also been helped by the observation of leadership trainer James Lawrence, who says that a good way of determining our greatest talents is noticing 'what you can't help yourself doing.'[7]

Personally, I cannot stop myself from sensing and then trying to solve any structural or people problems in any organisation I'm part of. My mum recently asked me whether I've ever seen one and not felt I need to get it sorted – and I struggled to think of an example. There is, obviously, a potential unhealthy Messiah complex in that,[8] but there is also a helpful indication of the gifts God has given me and the contexts in which they should be used.

I'm typing these words on a period of study leave and, to be honest, time away from the organisations, the church and charity, and the people I work for and with is making me miserable. I want to be back leading meetings, looking after staff, talking through problems, preaching sermons, training others and doing multiple things that are not spending all of my time in a library writing a book. But it's strangely reassuring to feel the pain of separation from those people and activities because it shows that I've found my sweet spot in doing what I'm doing with my life.

Writer Frederick Buechner says that we should all, as much as is possible, be seeking our answer to this question: 'At what points do my talents and deep gladness meet the world's deep need?'[9] In the delight my normal life gives me, the multiple opportunities to use the gifts God has given me, and the ways he is using them to meet the needs of people locally and further afield, I think that I've found my personal answer to that question.

What about you?

---

[7] James Lawrence in Nay Dawson, *She Needs: Women Flourishing in the Church* (London: IVP UK, 2024), p. 20.

[8] Apologies to everyone who has worked with me. And, again, for my tendency towards self-deprecation.

[9] Frederick Buechner in David Brooks, *The Road to Character* (London: Allen Lane, 2015), p. 22.

Sharing your woundedness

Enjoying intimacy with yourself is not all about enjoying using your strengths and connecting just with them. To be genuinely Christian, it also needs to be about learning to enjoy God using your weaknesses and your pain. The market leader in this is the apostle Paul, and the place to see this in action is his second letter to the Corinthians. It opens with these words:

> Praise be to the God and Father of our Lord Jesus Christ, the Father of compassion and the God of all comfort, who comforts us in all our troubles, so that we can comfort those in any trouble with the comfort we ourselves receive from God. For just as we share abundantly in the sufferings of Christ, so also our comfort abounds through Christ. If we are distressed, it is for your comfort and salvation; if we are comforted, it is for your comfort, which produces in you patient endurance of the same sufferings we suffer. And our hope for you is firm, because we know that just as you share in our sufferings, so also you share in our comfort.
> (2 Corinthians 1:3–8)

For him, Christian ministry – life – is like a game of pass the parcel: you pass on to others who are suffering what God has given you to keep you going in your sufferings. It's really 'pass the comfort'. You take what has most helped you, and you use it to help others. That is what Paul goes on to do in the rest of his letter, talking at length about his hard times, the trials he has been through, the weaknesses he has and the wounds he bears, so he can also talk about how Jesus has helped to keep him going through them all. I cannot tell you how many people I know, myself included, who have been kept going as Christians through Paul's bravery in sharing his own sense of woundedness. I say 'bravery' because his opponents in the Corinthian church despise him for his weaknesses, but he delights in them because he knows that sharing them will help others to keep going like him.

The Intimacy Deficit

As a result, I wonder if it's important for us not just to ask Buechner's 'At what points do my talents and deep gladness meet the world's deep need?' but also, 'At what point do my weaknesses and deep pain meet the world's deep need?' The good news is that working out what these are will probably take less time and conversation, and the potential power in sharing them with others and passing on how Jesus has comforted you in the context of them could be life-saving for some (yourself included).

For me, experiencing and enjoying intimacy with myself has meant connecting with some of my greatest wounds and recognising them, for good or ill, as part of me. My struggles with my sexuality and masculinity have long been the most painful parts of my life, but seeing them as, somehow, part of God's knitting together of me, as part of his plan, has been so important in making me feel increasingly at home in my body and at one with myself and him. Again, the puritan pastor John Flavel has most helped me here:

> All providences are overruled and ordered for good according to that blessed promise (Rom. 8.28); not only things that are good in themselves, as ordinances, graces, duties and mercies, but things that are evil in themselves, as temptations, afflictions, and even their sins and corruptions, shall turn in the issue to their advantage and benefit. For though sin is so intrinsically and formally evil in its own nature, then in itself it is not capable of sanctification, yet out of this worst of evils God can work good to His people. And though He never makes sin the instrument of good, yet His providence may make it the occasion of good to his people, so that spiritual benefits may, by the wise overruling of Providence, be occasioned by it.[10]

My desire to have sex with a man and my lack of contentment in being a man are sins that have afflicted me for all of my adult life.

---

[10] John Flavel, *The Mystery of Providence* (Edinburgh: Banner of Truth, 1963), p. 198.

And yet God has taken these wounds and used them for the good of me and others: to help me to see my need for God's mercy and grace, to help me to reorder my desires, to help others in their similar – and completely different – struggles with themselves and sin. Part of enjoying intimacy with myself has been slowly beginning to rejoice in these weaknesses, not just my strengths.

Remembering whose you are

Enjoying intimacy with myself is most possible when my view of myself and my identity has been grounded in *whose* I am rather than my struggles with *who* I am. I regularly return to some of the Bible verses we looked at in the previous chapter to remind myself of what is true of me despite my sin, my wounds and my weaknesses. Those painful realities don't change the spiritual reality that I am his divinely imaged creature, united to his perfect Son and gifted by his Holy Spirit. These biblical facts are solid foundations that give me a sense of self to delight in even when my woundedness feels overwhelming.

I recommend collecting one or two of the Bible verses or phrases that God's Spirit has most used to remind you whose you are and learning them by heart (which is, of course, one of the best ways of connecting them *to* your heart). You can then deploy them in those moments when your apparent lack of the right personality and gifts, or the prominence of your weaknesses and failures, is in danger of defining you more than anything else. To be able to say words like these to yourself can be spiritually life-saving: 'I live by faith in the Son of God, who loved me and gave himself for me' (Galatians 2:20).

The relational intimacy of these words, the sense of connection with Jesus that Paul is expressing, is just the right divine medicine when what we are saying about ourselves is overwhelmingly negative (and sometimes when others are saying it, too). Our ultimate value comes from Jesus' love for us and what he was willing to give for us, which was, of course, his very self. Nothing gives you – and me – more value than him.

Encouragement to intimacy with yourself

The road to enjoying intimacy with yourself might seem a little too rocky and steep, but it's crucial because of the knock-on effects. Christian psychiatrist Pablo Martinez points out that:

> The necessary requisite for us to be able to approach others adequately is a healthy concept of personal identity. The development of intimacy in relationships will depend upon the security that one has in oneself. The more unsure a person is, the more relational conflicts the person will have. The poorer the person's self-image, the greater the difficulty in becoming close to others. Deep down, people who have relational problems with others have not learned to relate well to themselves. They are in conflict with others because of the conflict with themselves.
>
> The result of all of this will be problems in having an intimate relationship with God. They will find it difficult to trust in God because it is difficult for them to trust in themselves.[11]

Intimacy with yourself is as crucial to where we'll turn next – intimacy with others – as it was to where we started – intimacy with God. Learning slowly, perhaps painfully, to say Psalm 139:13–18 to God about yourself is something we all need to do for the wider relational benefits it will bring.

This helps to make the point – an important one at this stage of the book – that none of these four main God-given contexts for intimacy stand alone: they need each other. A deepening intimacy with God needs a growing intimacy with yourself, but as we've discovered, true intimacy with yourself is founded on knowing that you belong to him. As a result, our intimacy deficit cannot be solved sequentially – 'I've achieved intimacy with God, I will now turn to delighting in myself, before better connecting with other

---

11 Pablo Martinez, *Praying with the Grain: How Your Personality Affects the Way You Pray* (Oxford: Monarch, 2012), p. 105.

people!' Instead, we need to be working, empowered by God's Spirit, on deepening our intimacy in all four contexts at the same time, knowing that they happily reinforce each other.

Keep on reading to get the full picture, and keep on praying for God's help in solving our intimacy deficit.

Intimacy with yourself: questions for reflection and discussion

- What is intimacy with yourself?
- Why is it so foundational to know *whose* you are?
- What stops you from enjoying intimacy with yourself?
- What do you most need in place to better enjoy it?
- How could that happen?

Further reading

Graham Beynon, *Mirror, Mirror: Discover Your True Identity in Christ* (London: IVP UK, 2008).

5
Intimacy with others

> The single most common finding from a half century's research on the correlates of life satisfaction, not only in the United States but around the world is that happiness is best predicted by the breadth and depth of one's social connections.[1]
> Robert Putnam

Jolsna's question

The leaders of the family of churches I'm part of have a much-repeated question. We call it 'the Jolsna Question' after the person who first got us asking it whenever anyone was struggling with life in general. The question is this: 'Who are their friends?' All too often, the answer is just a long silence, which helps to explain the struggle and is nearly always a big part of the solution: finding them some good friends.

Professor Robert Putnam's academic research would confirm this, as would my experience. I know that I most struggle in life when I've distanced myself from my friends, when I lack community. There are times when I'm away from home too much, when I haven't made the time for a proper conversation with a good friend for far too long, and the result is a loneliness that descends like a fog. I feel an intimacy deficit, disconnected from the people who know and love me best. My mood goes downhill and, often, I begin a disastrous search for false intimacy in less than godly ways.

---

[1] Robert Putnam in Iain McGilchrist, *The Master and His Emissary: The Divided Brain and the Making of the Western World* (New Haven, CT: Yale University Press, 2010), p. 435.

Intimacy with others

We all need to experience intimacy with God, ourselves *and* other people. It turns out that a world in which we existed by ourselves, with just God for company, would not be good for us. How do we know that? Because those sorts of conditions once existed. The world was populated by one man, Adam, in perfect relationship with God himself, and this was God's assessment of the situation: 'The LORD God said, "It is not good for the man to be alone. I will make a helper suitable for him"'(Genesis 2:18). This is perhaps a shock to us: God says that he alone is not enough to meet all of our intimacy needs. Our Creator designed us to need close relationships with his other creatures too – and not just one person of the opposite sex but whole families and communities. Eve is created next not as *the* solution to Adam's intimacy deficit but as the source, with him, of all the different sorts of relationships each of us – single or married – need. To flourish, every human being must be part of a whole network of intimate relationships, and that is what God begins to make possible here.

I'm going to focus our talk of intimacy with others on friendship because it's open to all of us. As we do this, we need to recognise that any reliance on friendships rather than family to meet our intimacy needs is too often seen as the booby prize for anyone who has failed to find 'the one' who will properly complete them. But no individual person can end our intimacy deficit alone and, too often, nuclear families collapse under the pressure to meet all of its members' relational needs. Journalist Andrew Sullivan observes that:

> Families and marriages fail too often because they are trying to answer too many human needs. A spouse is required to be a lover, a friend, a mother, a father, a soulmate, a co-worker, and so on. Few people can be all these things for one person. And when demands are set too high, disappointment can only follow. If husbands and wives have deeper and stronger friendships outside the marital unit, the marriage has more space to breathe and fewer burdens to bear.[2]

---

[2] Andrew Sullivan, *Love Undetectable: Notes on Friendship, Sex, and Survival* (London: Vintage, 1999), p. 234.

We all need close friendships. That might include a friend we're married to, but we don't need to be married to thrive in life. Just remember Jesus: the greatest example of what it is to be human, and a single man at the heart of a whole network of friendships that met his intimacy needs.

Jesus' need for friendships with other human beings, alongside his intimate relationship with his Father in heaven, should be a massive encouragement for us to build similar relationships. It turns out that it is not Christian to think that all we need in life is him. He knows, from personal experience, that human beings need other human beings too. As a result, pastor Dietrich Bonhoeffer writes:

> The believer feels no shame, as though he were still living too much in the flesh, when he yearns for the physical presence of other Christians. Man was created a body, the Son of God appeared on earth in the body, he was raised in the body, in the sacrament receives the Lord Jesus in the body, and the resurrection of the dead will bring about the perfected fellowship of God's spiritual-physical creatures. The believer therefore lauds the Creator, the Redeemer, God, Father, Son and Holy Spirit, for the bodily presence of a brother.[3]

Those words were a great comfort to me during the first Covid lockdown when I was physically alone for months. Yes, Jesus was with me by his Spirit in a way no one else could be, and I was so grateful for that spiritual reality, but I wasn't wrong to want to experience the physical presence of other human beings too. We've been created to enjoy not only a friendship with God but also friendships with others.

Biblical friendships

The full range of friendships the Bible portrays and encourages is too often forgotten, and just a few isolated proverbs are quoted. I

---

3 Dietrich Bonhoeffer, *Life Together* (London: SCM, 1954), p. 9.

want us to see the different sorts of friendships we find in Scripture (the focus of the rest of this chapter) so we might impersonate the best of them in our daily lives (the more practical focus of the next).

Same-sex friendships

I love these deliberately provocative words from Rebecca McLaughlin:

> People sometimes say the Bible condemns same-sex relationships. It does not. The Bible *commands* same-sex relationships at a level of intimacy that Christians seldom reach. Jesus preached a gospel of radical intimacy: with him first and foremost, but through him also with each other.[4]

If you're a woman reading these words, then you need some close female friends. If you're a man, then you need to feel a real, deep connection with some of the men in your life. But if gender stereotypes are accurate (and they often contain more than a kernel of truth), women will likely know this kind of experience more commonly than men.

The life of Jesus should correct any sense among men that same-sex intimacy is not needed. The Gospels clearly portray a particular closeness that Jesus enjoyed with an inner group of the twelve disciples (Peter, James and John) and a special connection with one of them ('the disciple whom Jesus loved'[5]). The intimacy of Jesus' relationship with John is most clearly communicated in his words entrusting his mother Mary to John's care (see John 19:25–27). This is a good test of a close friendship: do you have someone in your life whom you could ask to take care of your mum if you died prematurely? If you do, then you have the sort of friendship that Jesus needed and that you and I need too.

Of course, it is not just Jesus and John who provide biblical encouragement for close same-sex friendships. In the Old

---

4 McLaughlin, *Confronting Christianity*, p. 155. Emphasis original.
5 A description used by John himself in John 13:23, 19:26, 21:7 and 21:20.

Testament, there is a similar deep connection: the intimacy in the relationship between David and Jonathan. Here is David's response to hearing of Jonathan's death:

> I grieve for you, Jonathan my brother;
>   you were very dear to me.
> Your love for me was wonderful,
>   more wonderful than that of women.
> (2 Samuel 1:26)

These are striking words for many to read today – men whose only intimate relationship has been with their wives, or those who cannot conceive of a love deeper than the romantic connection between a man and a woman. A contemporary 'Queer' reading of David's words inevitably sees his relationship with Jonathan as having been sexual, but there is not a shred of evidence for that in anything else we are told about them – just a depth of love for each other that puts modern definitions and experiences of friendship to shame.

The beauty of the words that determine the relationship between Naomi and Ruth are also a victim of our modern sexualisation of all relationships, but they should be read as a great expression of a true, deep kinship or friendship.

> Where you go I will go, and where you stay I will stay. Your people will be my people and your God my God. Where you die I will die, and there I will be buried. May the LORD deal with me, be it ever so severely, if even death separates you and me.
> (Ruth 1:16–17)

The intimacy of good same-sex friendships is encapsulated so movingly in promises like these, in David's grief for Jonathan and in Jesus' trust in John. They should inspire us to seek the same depth in our friendships, unencumbered by the harmful, sex-obsessed interpretations of such relationships in our culture today.

Opposite-sex friendships

It is not just the same sex that we should be seeking relational intimacy with: opposite-sex friendships are also commended in the Scriptures. One of these friendships might be with the person we get married to (an existing friendship is, of course, one of the best foundations for a good marriage), but they don't need to be limited to just our husband or wife.

This is controversial, but Jesus wasn't afraid of wading into controversy if it would be good for his people. The gospel accounts, counter-culturally, show us that Jesus enjoyed several close relationships with women. I love how his relationship with one of them, Mary Magdalene, is intimately portrayed in one of the resurrection accounts in John 20. A weeping Mary is devastated by the discovery of Jesus' empty tomb – what have they done with him now? The resurrected Jesus appears by her side, but she doesn't recognise who he is until he calls her by her name. It's the intimacy of that act, her recognising his voice saying 'Mary' (see John 20:16), that makes her recognise him. And then what does she want to do immediately? She hugs him. Touch is a natural part of their close relationship – Jesus has to tell her not to on this occasion (see John 20:17). She has clearly been held by him before.

But to be alone with a woman today, to be held by one, is against the rules in many Christian subcultures. Opposite-sex friendships, beyond someone you could be or are married to, are frowned upon and seen as a context for immorality. In his book on opposite-sex friendships, Dan Brennan writes:

> In my thirty years of attending churches I have heard two narratives in Christian communities: 1) the marital/ romantic story, and 2) the danger story. Both stories of course, involve an introduction, a plot, and a climax towards the same thing: sex.[6]

---

6 Dan Brennan, *Sacred Union, Sacred Passions: Engaging the Mystery of Friendship Between Men and Women* (Elgin, IL: Faith Dance Publishing, 2010), p. 56.

Jesus' close friendships with women like Mary Magdalene contradict both narratives. It's possible for our opposite-sex friendships to do the same too. Author Aimee Byrd gives good advice:

> Of course we promote one another's holiness, take sin seriously, and realise that we can easily fall into it. We don't think of a bunch of reasons to be alone with the other sex, we don't naively assume that everyone is safe, and we don't overestimate our own virtue. But, rather than creating extra-biblical rules, we are to do the hard work of rightly orientating our affections and exercising wisdom and discernment with others. We live before God in every situation. And in this manner, we will be able to perform ordinary acts of kindness and business without scandal.[7]

The apostle Paul clearly managed this, as his list of male and female co-workers in Romans 16 demonstrates. His advice to the young pastor Timothy is not to avoid women but instead to treat everyone in the church like family members:

> Do not rebuke an older man harshly, but exhort him as if he were your father. Treat younger men as brothers, older women as mothers, and younger women as sisters, with absolute purity.
> (1 Timothy 5:1–2)

Good, appropriate opposite-sex friendships should be part of all our lives today. They might have different boundaries based on our personal circumstances and godliness challenges, but our friendships with the opposite sex shouldn't be limited to our husband or wife, or someone we're auditioning for that role.

---

[7] Aimee Byrd, *Why Can't We Be Friends? Avoidance Is Not Purity* (Phillipsburg, NJ: P&R, 2018), p. 77.

Intergenerational friendships

The Bible also portrays some beautifully healthy intergenerational friendships.[8] Naomi and Ruth are an example of this, as are Paul and his young friends Timothy and Titus. James K. A. Smith rightly recommends relationships between young and old for the benefit of both parties:

> If you want to transcend time, build friendships across generations. Though you can't stand outside your own season, you can hear from those who've lived through your season. In my experience this is one of the great gifts of multigenerational friendships. Friendship in this respect is akin to time travel … if we can relinquish the myth of utter singularity, then listening to those generations ahead of us is a way of learning from our future. Granted it is the nature of youth to spurn such gifts. But when we are humbled, friendship across the generations becomes a lifeline, an almost sacramental means of transcending the purview of our now as God gives us an outside glimpse of our moment. But the gifts traverse time both ways. Older generations attentively listening to those younger avail themselves of different ears to hear what's whispering or shouting now.[9]

I've so benefitted from the friendships I've enjoyed with people of my parents' generation (and older). Years ago, I asked a friend in her eighties how she was still so energised by life. 'Young friends!' was her answer.

Church communities can be one of the few places in our Western societies where young and old mix on a weekly basis. Make the most of this mix by developing deep friendships with those who have been through and completed the stage or circumstances of

---

8 For more help on what makes such relationships healthy, and the challenge of imbalanced power dynamics making them unhealthy, read John Wyatt, *Transforming Friendship: Lessons from John Stott & Others* (London: IVP UK, 2023).
9 James K. A. Smith in John Wyatt, *Transforming Friendship*, p. 113.

life you're travelling through, or who could benefit by learning from the mistakes you made and/or the opportunities you made the most of.

Diverse friendships

The names recorded in the New Testament epistles testify to the racial diversity of the early church, and the teaching they contain for both slaves and masters points to the differences in class, economic and educational backgrounds among the first believers. As Christians, we believe that we are heading to a point when we will be part of 'a great multitude, that no one can count, from every nation, tribe, people, and language' (Revelation 7:9). A good way of getting ready for that day of the greatest of unity in the middle of the greatest of diversity is embracing difference in our friendships in the here and now.

Seeking friends who are just like us – from the same place or background, with the same opportunities – is very limiting for both them and us. Instead, we should be on the lookout for difference because, as theologian Ephraim Radner observes, 'In all friendships of depth there is always the realization of the glorious victory of difference over likeness.'[10] No computer algorithm would have matched me with many of my best friends. The real connection comes not from any similarity but our complementarity.

Church implications

Before (in the next chapter) we think through the practical implications for us individually, let's dwell on a couple of implications the importance of intimacy with others has for our church family lives together.

---

10 Ephraim Radner, *A Time to Keep: Theology, Mortality and the Shape of Human Life* (Waco, TX: Baylor University Press, 2016), p. 184.

Christian ministry is about encouraging friendships

When training staff or small group leaders at my church, I often encourage them to see one of their primary roles as being friendship catalysts, enabling those they are caring for to build deep, intimate relationships with others. One of the great dangers I've kept falling into in my ministry is thinking that I need to help everyone myself rather than assisting God in making the connections between different people that will most help them to grasp his love and share that love with others. As pastor Jonathan Grant points out:

> The church is one of the few remaining social spaces where people can come together with the express intention of forming loving friendships without the constant pressure of sexual connection. As Christian ministers, we can play an influential role within this dynamic by encouraging genuine communities of friendship in practice. Part of our task is to ask whether we are promoting social spaces and ministry contexts in which people's fundamental needs for relational intimacy are being met, as well as opportunities for people to express their affective (social) sexuality in line with its divine purpose.[11]

The night before I wrote this chapter, I was speaking to a friend whose current church family did this so well. Right from her first Sunday, there were multiple opportunities, invitations and contexts for her to build the close friendships that have helped her to thrive as a single Christian in her thirties. She was so grateful.

---

11 Jonathan Grant, *Divine Sex: A Compelling Vision for Christian Relationships in a Hypersexualized Age* (Ada, MI: Brazos, 2015), p. 234.

Those without friends shouldn't be Christian ministers

Another implication of the importance of enjoying intimacy with others is this: you shouldn't be in ministry if you aren't enjoying friendship yourself. Many parts of the UK church are reeling from scandals in which prominent leaders have sought inappropriate control over the lives of others, including unhealthy intimacy with younger men. In this context, author John Wyatt helpfully points us to this insight from Catholic priest Henri Nouwen:

> One thing is clear to me: the temptation of power is greatest when intimacy is a threat. Much Christian leadership is exercised by people who do not know how to develop healthy, intimate relationships and have opted for power and control instead. Many Christian empire-builders have been people unable to give and receive love.[12]

If the people we're considering for church leadership don't have friends – people they deeply connect to in life-giving, positive ways – we should be wary of appointing them.

So many of the attributes Paul trains us to look for in the pastoral epistles (see, in particular, 1 Timothy 3:1–7 and Titus 1:5–9) are relational skills, things that are needed to build appropriately intimate relationships in which any power is used to serve others rather than dominate them. Too often, the ability to teach and the up-front presentational skills someone demonstrates dazzle us, so we fail to notice the lack of any real relational connection, which is so damaging for them and others. If only people had asked Jolsna's question, 'Who are their friends?', a lot of pain and damage might have been avoided.

---

12 Henri J. M. Nouwen in Wyatt, *Transforming Friendship*, p. 119.

6
Enjoying intimacy with others

> What does more to stay us and keep our backbones stiff while the world reels around us than the sense that we are linked with someone who listens and understands and so in some way completes us?[1]
> *Wallace Stegner*

Blockers to intimacy with others

So, who are *your* friends? Who are the people who, in novelist Wallace Stegner's words, complete you? Remember Tim Keller's definition of true friendship: 'There are two features of real friendship – constancy and transparency. Real friends always let you in, and they never let you down.'[2] Who fits that description in your life? Do you meet that definition yourself? It's quite a tall order! But if no one does, it is, as we saw in the previous chapter, a real problem.

All of us need to be and have a few real, intimate friends. Varying circumstances and personalities will shape the pattern and number of them – some of us will have more, others less – but we should all be continually seeking to be the sort of friend who meets this high bar and looking for friends who will do the same for us. Sadly, there are several things that regularly stop that from happening.

---

[1] Page Stegner (ed), *The Selected Letters of Wallace Stegner* (Berkeley, CA: Counterpoint, 2007), p. i.
[2] Keller, *The Meaning of Marriage*, p. 112.

Fear

Writer Elaine Storkey captures this so well:

> Intimacy is both desired and threatening. We both want our deepest privacy to be invaded, but we also fear it. We want to be able to open up our very selves to the love and scrutiny of another, yet we dread the rawness of being exposed. There is somehow deep in the human psyche that tension between bonding and detachment, closeness and distance. Very often, just at the very point where intimacy seems realizable there is a fear of being engulfed, a claustrophobia, a panic and a bid for retreat. To accept that this tension is there, and to live creatively with it are probably marks of maturity. But for many the fear of intimacy itself can take over. The unwillingness to be completely open to another lies deeply in our personhood. How can we ever really trust each other to disclose our hearts and show all the weakness there?[3]

This will especially be the case for those of us who have sought to be there for others, opened ourselves up to them in the past, made sacrifices, been vulnerable, and have then been ignored, unappreciated or even betrayed. Fear is understandably strongest when our worst fears have already been realised.

But even if that is not our history, giving or sharing ourselves is a big step. We've probably all had those moments when we were about to disclose something significant and painful with someone else for the very first time and then bottled it at the last moment, thinking 'How will they respond?' or, 'Will they want to be my friend anymore?' We instinctively protect ourselves, and sometimes it can feel like the best way of doing that is by not letting anyone else in. Our fears constrain us.

---

3 Storkey, *The Search for Intimacy*, p. 2.

Pride

Pride can also get in the way. We live in an age when maturity is often seen as self-sufficiency and immaturity as dependence on others. Bishop FitzSimons Allison writes:

> There seems to be some dynamic in us all that resists ever needing, or being in any way dependent on, another. It is the cause of much of our loneliness, and our shallow and inadequate friendships.[4]

As a result, we find it hard to articulate our needs to others, to be honest and open. To ring a friend and say, 'I really need some company tonight!' would seem too needy. We would prefer to suffer in silence than let someone else know that we aren't really coping with life.

Masculinity

Many men, in particular, have been discouraged from developing a healthy biblical pattern of dependence *on* others by harmful cultural visions of masculine independence *from* others. In traditional cultures, a true man is often portrayed as self-sufficient and not relationally needy. Alongside this false narrative, more and more men are now using up their leisure time in more individualistic activities than previous generations – like on screens, at the gym or out jogging. All of this makes me feel that my friend Rachel Gilson has a point when she half-jokingly says, 'Jesus' greatest miracle was that he was a man in his thirties with twelve close friends.'[5]

Her words always make me laugh, but they should, potentially, make us cry. Perhaps talk of intimate friendship does make you want to weep. Perhaps you know that you need it, but everything about the world in which you live undermines it: the attitudes,

---

4 C. FitzSimons Allison, *The Cruelty of Heresy: An Affirmation of Christian Orthodoxy* (London: SPCK, 1994), p. 91.

5 'Meet the Authors 13: Rachel Gilson', *Living Out* Podcast, 1 July 2021, https://www.livingout.org/resources/podcasts/24/meet-the-authors-13-rachel-gilson.

your hobbies, the constant banter. If that's you, a vision of Jesus as the true man, the great definition of masculinity, at the heart of a network of friendships with other men and women should be an encouragement to change. It might help you to make a practical change by embracing activities you can do alongside other men – team sports, watching a boxset together, walking with others, second-hand book shopping (the latter works best for me). For some reason, men are (generally) better at connecting when doing something together, so plan the joint activities that might allow your male friendships to grow.

Romanticism

Some authors make friendship forming sound like a Hollywood romance. They talk of a moment when you suddenly discover a shared interest or a real connection and a friendship blossoms effortlessly. That does happen sometimes, but most friendships need to be worked at. They come from working together on something and not from spontaneously clicking with someone else. In myself and others, I sometimes detect a laziness that might be fuelling this romantic ideal. Writer Roger Deakin once wrote:

> I want all my friends to come up like weeds, and I want to be a weed myself, spontaneous and unstoppable. I don't want the kind of friends one has to cultivate.[6]

I get the appeal of this, but I suspect that the result would be plenty of acquaintances but a lack of friends, because real friendship takes effort. Constancy and transparency aren't easy for any of us.

Perfectionism

I know that I'm a bit of a perfectionist when it comes to friendships. I have high standards, and I don't like it when people fail to meet them. I'm very good at dumping a friend the first time they let me down or when I discover something I don't like about them.

---

6 Roger Deakin, *Notes from Walnut Tree Farm* (London: Penguin, 2009), p. 63.

I'm not good at working through misunderstandings or conflict, at showing forgiveness (despite so constantly needing it myself). I was massively rebuked a few years back by these words from Francis Schaeffer: 'If we demand, in any of our relationships, either perfection or nothing, we will get nothing.'[7]

I can, sadly, think of people who have no real friends because no one has quite passed muster. When I feel tempted to let someone go because they have disappointed me in some way, I need to stop myself, especially because no one would befriend me if they insisted on perfection too!

Moving

I always encourage people to stick in one place for as long as possible, as soon as possible. Too often today, deep friendships are undermined by educational and career choices that result in people moving just as real intimacy starts to develop. You finally get to that moment when you can trust someone, and either they or you are off to a new city, church or job. With more and more people working from home and more and more entertainment available in the home, opportunities for friendship building are getting rarer, which only makes things harder. The impact on a generation's general well-being is seen in ever-increasing feelings of isolation, which are contributing hugely to our Western mental health crisis.

If you want to enjoy intimacy with others, you need to pick a place, a community, to be part of as soon as you can and get involved in it as much as you can. If necessary, sacrifice other good things like that new experience, that promotion or that better school for the kids to stay in a place where a network of deep relationships is developing.

One of the great blessings I've experienced is that of living and working in the same city for over twenty years. I have a network of people who know me intimately as a result of me (and them) staying put. Many of my contemporaries, who have moved three or five times in the same period, do not. I have one friend in the

---

7 Francis Schaeffer, *No Little People* (Wheaton, IL: Crossway, 2003), p. 51.

armed forces who, on one level, has sacrificed a lot in not dragging his family around the country (and the world) with each new posting, but he has gained a lot by giving them, and himself, a place where they are known and loved and can know and love others themselves. I know that this won't always be possible, and that the gospel itself compels some of us to move places, even countries, to share Jesus in word and deed with those in need, but even then, the encouragement to stay put as much as possible would benefit both our friendships and our evangelism.

Busyness

My drug of choice for coping with loneliness in life is to fill my time with work and ministry. The problem is that doing so leaves no time for friendship and discourages people from reaching out to me because I seem so busy. They, very kindly, don't want to bother me, when the greatest kindness they could do for me would be to drag me away from my never-ending, self-inflicted list of things to do and people to see. This is a vicious cycle that has increased my intimacy deficit so often and has only been broken when the loneliness has got too much, or there has been a merciful intervention by friends who know me only too well.

I know that I am (ironically) not alone in this, and I suspect that others keep themselves busy to avoid the painful feelings of loneliness that can be much-needed catalysts for committing to growing our intimacy with others. They are red lights flashing on the dashboard of our lives. Let's turn now to see what else might help.

Catalysts for intimacy with others

If truly deep friendships are about constancy and transparency, they will involve two things: intentionality and vulnerability.

Intentionality

You have to make friendships happen. Give time, develop habits and make choices that give relational intimacy the time to grow, and ensure that you're there for others. Intimate friendships need to be cultivated, and maintaining a good network of them is like gardening: there is planning, planting, watering, waiting, harvesting and pruning to be done all the time. Neglect the garden for a while and you're in trouble. Put in the hard work, and both you and your friends will reap the benefits.

If you're thinking, 'I don't have the time for that!', you do. You need to make the time to thrive in life and to help others to thrive too. It will involve being intentional, looking at your diary and seeing what time you can share with others to build deeper relationships with them. It doesn't necessarily mean finding space for new activities, just deliberately doing existing things with others and (perhaps) expecting them to take slightly longer as a result. You must eat, and you have (I hope!) been making the time to do that for years. Now, plan to eat more with others – invite people round, eat your packed lunches together near work or go out for food with people. You have, I trust, got into the habit of serving at church. Now, make sure you're serving on a team that gives you the chance to get alongside people and get to know them better. You have holidays to take. Now, choose to go on them with others – not just people who will be good company but people you want to love and care for.

Examining my deepest friendships, I see that they are with people I've regularly shared meals with. There is something strangely intimacy producing about eating with others. With some friends, this has meant a regular meal every week or two, or always getting the next date in the diary. Sometimes, I've formed friendships with those I've served alongside at church, leading a weekly area of ministry together or serving on the same rota at the same time (the more challenging the context of service, the better we've got to know each other). I've made friends with the people I head off on holiday with – I have three different combinations of friends I regularly go away with, and our annual times with one another undergird our friendships the rest of the year (one holiday is a city break, the other a family holiday, and the third is attending a Christian conference together). We haven't just waited for our friendships to deepen; we've intentionally sought to give them the time and space to grow and acted as friendship catalysts in one another's lives.

This has sometimes involved making lists of everyone I know, choosing whom I will prioritise (for my sake and theirs), and then establishing the habits that will see me follow through on those decisions. This can sound very clinical, but I have made the common mistake of having too many friends and trying to catch up with them all to the point where I don't have the time to be truly connected and genuinely close with any of them. Having, at times, really felt the lack of friends who truly know how I am, I know that I need to see a few people on a regular basis to share the ups and downs of our lives together effectively. Sometimes, this happens naturally because we live or work in the same place (my university years were the easiest), but if we don't, it takes a real intentionality and a degree of exclusivity. With my friends Emily and Alasdair, and with my friend Phil, I've established a pattern of getting regular dates in the diary to see each other at the beginning of each term. When we haven't done that, the time between our meet-ups has drifted apart, and we've started to drift apart too.

If you don't have any of the above in place already, you need to be proactive – as intentional as a friend of mine who approached a few people at his church saying that he needed some closer friends, sharing what that might look like, and asking if they would be up for it. That sort of intentionality took some guts, but – wonderfully – it was God's way of reducing the intimacy deficit in his life *and* in the lives of others who were feeling the same need but weren't quite as courageous in doing something about it as him.

One of the reasons we have to be so intentional is that there are different seasons of life. People and their circumstances change. There was a lovely patch for me when a good friend and I had the opportunity to speak for an hour every Friday lunchtime – it was an easy day for me, and he was between jobs. Friday now doesn't work for me, and he's working again. That change was always going to happen, but there is an intimacy deficit in my life as a result. I need to register that and intentionally come up with a new way of remaining closely connected to him, or I need to seek a new connection with someone else.

'But what about spontaneity?' some will be crying! It still has its place in building friendships – often at the very beginning as you invite that new person to come with you on the walk, or to join other friends for a drink. It can play a big part when you're new to a place, or at stages of life when you have a lot of free time and few responsibilities. But as lives get more settled and busier, intentionality is a better friend of friendship than spontaneity. I'm not saying that the spontaneous trip to the cinema has no place (a few middle-aged friends did this recently, calculating that it was about twenty years since we'd spontaneously done anything together), but in our crowded modern lives, intentionality is increasingly the key to enjoying intimacy with others.

Vulnerability

You can plan to meet up with someone every day of your life and still miss out on true intimacy, real connection, if you aren't willing to be vulnerable and transparent with them. Author Justin Whitmel Earley coaches us on this:

> Vulnerability and time turn people who have relationship into a people who have a friendship. That's what friendship is: vulnerability across time. The practice of conversation is the basis of friendship because it's in the conversation that we become exposed to each other.[8]

If you want to enjoy true intimacy with others, then you need to make time for them intentionally. When you're with them, you need to talk about what's really going on in your lives. This is a massive challenge for so many of us because, as writer Frederick Buechner accurately observes:

---

8 Justin Whitmel Earley, *The Common Rule: Habits of Purpose for an Age of Distraction* (San Francisco, CA: IVP USA, 2019), p. 98.

> When we are with other people, we are apt to talk about almost anything under the sun except for what really matters to us, except for our own lives, except for what is going on inside our own skins. We pass the time of day. We chatter. We hold each other at bay, keep our distance from each other even when God knows it is precisely each other that we desperately need.[9]

Doesn't this description feel familiar? Think of so many conversations we have with our friends. 'How are you?' they ask. We reply with the same question, but neither of us actually answers it. It's just an empty greeting, and we move on to the weather, sport or the kids. People's marriages collapse, others have nervous breakdowns, and their friends are shocked because no real communication ever took place before. We didn't give them the chance to raise the alarm.

How do we change this? We start telling the truth about our lives. David Brooks writes, 'Intimacy happens when somebody shares something emotionally meaningful, and the other person receives it and shares back.'[10] Wonderfully relational connection takes place when someone talks about something intimate (their feelings, fears or failures), and the other person responds in kind. It can be that straightforward. Intimacy breeds intimacy.

The times that have most quickly deepened friendships are those when I've replied to 'How are you?' with my anger, despair and tears – with the truth. And when people have responded by both listening carefully to my feelings *and* sharing their own, the listening has made me feel valued and the sharing has stopped me from feeling all alone.

I love this line from a novel by Andrew Sean Greer: 'I do not know what joins the parts of an atom, but it seems what binds one human being to another is pain.'[11] The mutual sharing of struggles – real vulnerability – creates intimacy like nothing else.

---

9 Frederick Buechner, *A Room Called Remember: Uncollected Pieces* (London: HarperCollins, 1992), p. 5.
10 Brooks, *The Second Mountain*, p. 151.
11 Andrew Sean Greer, *The Story of a Marriage* (London: Faber & Faber, 2011), p. 85.

There is a time and place. We don't need to spend our entire social lives sharing our deepest, darkest secrets. Sometimes, we choose the wrong moment or the wrong person – who runs a mile. But if you want to deepen your friendships, then share things you have buried deeply for years. Such intentionality and vulnerability will bring you the intimacy with others that we all, deep down, long for because we've been designed to need it.

All of this is hard work. It will be complicated, painful, messy. But getting it wrong can itself be a catalyst for intimacy. As writer Anne Lamott rightly observes, 'Rubble is the ground on which our deepest friendships are built.'[12] Some of my closest friendships are those that have survived times when the need for constancy and transparency, intentionality and vulnerability were forgotten, but then repentance (by me) and forgiveness (by them) have seen the friendship not just restored but deepened.

Encouragement to intimacy with others

Because all of this will be hard work, we need some final motivation. First of all, it's worth noting that Jesus did intentionality and vulnerability, saying to his inner group of disciples on the night before he laid down his life for them and us:

> I no longer call you servants, because a servant does not know his master's business. Instead, I have called you friends, for everything that I learned from my Father I have made known to you. You did not choose me, but I chose you and appointed you so that you might go and bear fruit – fruit that will last – and so that whatever you ask in my name the Father will give you.
> (John 15:15–16)

Jesus was open, transparent and vulnerable to them and for them, sharing everything his Father had shared with him. In choosing

---

12 Anne Lamott, *Plan B: Further Thoughts on Faith* (New York, NY: Riverhead, 2005), p. 174.

them, he had been very intentional: he had called them by name. They were not a spontaneous group of friends but a carefully curated one. The sort of friendship we should be offering others is one Jesus has already freely given us.

And then, it's worth remembering that intimacy with other Christians should be a catalyst for deeper intimacy with God. In his excellent book on friendship, John Wyatt helpfully quotes the medieval monk Bernard of Clairvaux, who wrote that, 'Christ himself kisses us in the love of our friends.'[13] The way we are most effectively and intimately connected with Jesus in the middle of our busy lives is often by the friend who hears about our pain, our doubts, our joys, our dreams, and helps us to feel and express them in the light of God's fatherly care, or by recommending a particular psalm to adopt, or by reminding us who we now are in Christ, or by helping us to see how God's Spirit has especially gifted us, or by taking the time to pray with and for us. All the intimacy in each of the four areas we are looking at should leak out and bring intimacy in all the others too.

Intimacy with others: questions for reflection and discussion

- What is intimacy with others?
- Why do we need it?
- What stops you from enjoying intimacy with others?
- What do you most need in place to better enjoy it?
- How could that happen?

Further reading

John Wyatt, *Transforming Friendship: Lessons from John Stott & Others* (London: IVP UK, 2023).

---

13 Bernard of Clairvaux in Wyatt, *Transforming Friendship*, p. 155.

7
Intimacy with Creation

Glory be to God for dappled things –
For skies of couple-colour as a brinded cow;
For rose-moles all in stipple upon trout that swim;
Fresh-firecoal chestnut-falls; finches' wings;
Landscape plotted and pieced – fold, fallow, and plough;
And áll trádes, their gear and tackle and trim.[1]
Gerard Manley Hopkins

Beauty appreciation

Take a moment to travel in your mind to the most beautiful place you've ever been. I don't know where you've ended up, but I'm on Herm Island.

Herm Island

Off the coast of Normandy are the Channel Islands, described by Victor Hugo, author of *Les Misérables*, as 'bits of France which fell into the sea and were picked up by England'.[2] As a result, everyone speaks English, but many of the street and place names are in French. I was born on the largest of them, Jersey, and my favourite place in the whole world is one of the smallest, Herm.

Herm is simply beautiful: it has long, sandy beaches and small coves, sheltered valleys and a windswept common, rugged cliff walks and beautifully kept gardens. I spend a couple of weeks there

---

1 Gerard Manley Hopkins, 'Pied Beauty'. https://www.poetryfoundation.org/poems/44399/pied-beauty.
2 Graham Robb, 'Victor Victorious', *The Guardian*, 2 March 2002, https://www.theguardian.com/education/2002/mar/02/artsandhumanities.highereducation.

annually, and I love every bit of the island, every moment I get to enjoy it.[3]

One morning each year, I get up early to watch the sunrise. I walk to one of the highest points on the island (Le Grand Monceau) with the dawn chorus beginning all around me, the air smelling so fresh and the dew wetting my feet. I look east towards the French coast, waiting for the sun to appear above the horizon. As it rises, I say these words to myself:

> The heavens declare the glory of God;
>   the skies proclaim the work of his hands.
> Day after day they pour forth speech;
>   night after night they reveal knowledge.
> They have no speech, they use no words;
>   no sound is heard from them.
> Yet their voice goes out into all the earth,
>   their words to the ends of the world.
> In the heavens God has pitched a tent for the sun.
>   It is like a bridegroom coming out of his chamber,
>   like a champion rejoicing to run his course.
> It rises at one end of the heavens
>   and makes its circuit to the other;
>   nothing is deprived of its warmth.
> (Psalm 19:1–6)

It is always an incredible experience to see the grandeur of God in his creation, to watch his sun begin to run its daily arc around the island, knowing that I'll be enjoying the western sunset at the end of the day. I often end up saying the psalm through my tears because the beauty of what I'm appreciating is overwhelming.

This past year, the sunrise was especially impressive. As I walked along the east coast of the island, I stopped at my favourite beach (Belvoir Bay) and, much to my surprise, found myself wanting to

---

[3] To get a taste of the beauty of the island, see https://www.herm.com/.

swim in the sea, which was beautifully illuminated by the rising sun.

Now, swimming in the sea is a very rare activity for me. I like to be warm, and I like to breathe. It was freezing, and I gasped for air, but I had felt compelled to plunge in. Why? C. S. Lewis helps me to make sense of that morning:

> We want something else which can hardly be put into words – to be united with the beauty we see, to pass into it, to receive it into ourselves, to bathe in it, to become part of it.[4]

I've felt the same listening to music, engrossed in a novel or admiring a building – that desire to stay connected, to become one with what I'm hearing or reading or seeing. This is what intimacy with creation is all about, and I hope that you've had a similar experience, though perhaps in a different context – watching a football match, at the ballet or on top of a mountain. Eugene Peterson joins C. S. Lewis in helping us to clock what's going on:

> In the presence of the beautiful we intuitively respond in delight, wanting to be involved, getting near, entering in – tapping our feet, humming along, touching, kissing, meditating, contemplating, imitating, believing, praying. It's the very nature of our five senses to pull us into whatever is there – scent, rhythm, texture, vision.[5]

Appreciating beauty in God's creation, in God's creatures, is something we've been wired to do. We cannot stop ourselves: it's an instinctive thing. This is why the writer Wendell Berry can describe this sort of moment like this: 'He did not say to himself that it was beautiful. He felt, he recognized, the beauty of it in his flesh.'[6]

---

[4] C. S. Lewis, 'The Weight of Glory' in *The C. S. Lewis Essay Collection: Faith, Christianity and the Church* (London: HarperCollins, 2002), p. 104.

[5] Eugene H. Peterson in DeWitt, *Eyes Wide Open*, p. 90.

[6] Wendell Berry, *How It Went: Thirteen More Stories of the Port William Membership* (Berkeley, CA: Counterpoint, 2022), p. 27.

Appreciating beauty is a very natural response, which God created us to enjoy in our very being. It's one of the most wonderful things about being alive.

Beauty boomerangs

This intimacy with creation, this instinctive connection with beauty, was at the heart of minister Jonathan Edwards's experience of life and worship of God in New England a few centuries ago. He made links many have been slow to make since. Here is an example:

> For as God is infinitely the greatest Being, so he is allowed to be infinitely the most beautiful and excellent: and all the beauty to be found throughout the whole creation is but the reflection of the diffused beams of that Being who hath an infinite fullness of brightness and glory; God ... is the foundation and fountain of all being and beauty.[7]

Developing the theology of Psalm 19 – what creation tells us about the Creator – Edwards encourages us to follow where beauty leads us: back to the source, our beautiful God, to bask in the beauty of God's Son as we enjoy the beauty of God's sun.

For Edwards, exploring, studying and enjoying the natural beauty of this world in all its complexity and detail (which he spent a lot of time doing) was of spiritual benefit:

> When we are delighted with flowery meadows and gentle breezes of wind, we may consider that we only see the emanations of the sweet benevolence of Jesus Christ; when we behold the fragrant rose and lily, we see his love and purity. So the green trees and fields, and singing of birds, are emanations of his infinite joy and benignity; the easiness and naturalness of trees and vines shadows of his infinite beauty

---

7 Jonathan Edwards in DeWitt, *Eyes Wide Open*, p. 18.

Intimacy with Creation

and loveliness; the crystal rivers and murmuring streams have the footsteps of his sweet grace and bounty.[8]

Here is someone who appreciated God's creation and grew in his appreciation of God through its beauty. He spent time getting to know creation more intimately so that, through it, he could know God more intimately. Pastor Steve DeWitt has come up with a lovely image to encapsulate all of this: 'Beauty boomerangs from God into created beauty, then through the senses and soul of the image-bearer, and finally back to God with praise and glory.'[9] This describes what beauty is meant to do, what effect creation should have on us: it should fuel our worship of the God who is behind it all.

Beauty creation

God doesn't just want us to appreciate beauty; he wants us to get involved in creating it too. He doesn't just want us to watch, listen or admire but to make it ourselves.

Creation mandate

This is made very clear right at the beginning of humanity when God gives people from all times and places a command through our representatives Adam and Eve:

> God blessed them and said to them, 'Be fruitful and increase in number; fill the earth and subdue it. Rule over the fish in the sea and the birds in the sky and over every living creature that moves on the ground.'
> (Genesis 1:28)

This is a commission, a mandate, that God has never rescinded. God still wants you and me to be getting on with these two tasks

---

[8] Jonathan Edwards in Lane, *Ravished by Beauty*, p. 177.
[9] DeWitt, *Eyes Wide Open*, p. 69.

today. We'll attempt to summarise them as 'making people' and 'making things'.

Making people

And I said this book wasn't about sex! But beauty creation does undeniably include the beauty of marriage and the beauty of marital sex, resulting – when possible – in the beauty of a newborn baby. Human beings having children, creating new life, is (whether people recognise it or not) an act of obedience to the very first command our Creator God gave us in Genesis 1:28.

Bringing children into this world and caring for them during their early years are clearly intimate acts that both require, and ideally create, deep connection between parents and child. Earlier in this book, we saw how God himself uses some of the tasks this involves as a living illustration of his intimate relationship with us as his children (see Hosea 11:1–4). Parents don't just make a child as a one-off event; they, ideally, continue to make their lives possible for years and decades after. Raising a child involves intimacy with creation, with a creature you'll come to know inside out.

But it also takes more than parents. Making children is not just a family business. I'm the biological product of Jonathan and Hazel Shaw (if they'll forgive me for putting it like that), but I'm also the product, the result, of the care of the rest of my family and our wider group of friends, the churches we were part of, my teachers at school, those who mentored me as a Christian – the list could go on and on. I've been made to be the person, the beautiful mess, I am today by a whole host of other people alongside my mum and dad.

This means that you can get involved in obeying the creation mandate even if you never have your own kids. As a single man, I haven't had a child. I don't have descendants on any biological family tree. But I do, for example, have spiritual children, people God has used me to make disciples of Jesus. Some of his people are people I've helped to make his people, and that is beauty creation too.

Justification of this wider application of Genesis 1:28 comes in the scholarly work of Greg Beale and Mitchell Kim as they compare the language of Genesis 1:28 with the words Luke uses in the New Testament book of Acts to describe the growth of God's people, the church:

> In Acts, the Genesis 1:28 language of 'be fruitful and multiply' marks the growth of the Church:
>
> > And the word of God continued *to be fruitful* and the number of disciples *multiplied* greatly in Jerusalem (Acts 6:7; our translation).
> >
> > But the word of God *bore fruit* and *multiplied* (Acts 12:24; our translation).
> >
> > So the word of the Lord continued to *bear fruit* and prevail mightily (Acts 19:20; our literal translation).
>
> ... Genesis 1:28 likely does not have in mind only physical children, but children who were also to be spiritual image bearers of God.[10]

All Christians are to get involved in helping to make people Christian – in spiritual parenting alongside biological parenting, for some. We should all be doing the beautifully intimate work of helping new or younger believers to learn to walk by themselves, comforting them when they fall and feeding them from God's word. When we do so, we are all helping to fulfil God's mandate of making people. And that is creating beauty: spreading more beauty throughout this world.

Making things

It is hard to encapsulate the second part of the creation mandate in a couple of words. Just to remind us, the whole thing reads like this:

---

10 G. K. Beale and Mitchell Kim, *God Dwells Among Us: Expanding Eden to the Ends of the Earth* (London: IVP UK, 2015), p. 36.

The Intimacy Deficit

> God blessed them and said to them, 'Be fruitful and increase in number; fill the earth and subdue it. Rule over the fish in the sea and the birds in the sky and over every living creature that moves on the ground.'
> (Genesis 1:28)

I think that 'making things' is a reasonable attempt at what filling, subduing and ruling the world looks like in practice – making laws, sausages, spreadsheets and infrastructure would all be good examples of what God tells us all to do here. We're to take his beautiful creation, care for it and develop it well, which includes those things (and many others too).

In his book on work, pastor Tim Keller helps us to see how wide-ranging this command of God's is:

> It is rearranging the raw material of God's creation in such a way that it helps the world in general, and people in particular, thrive and flourish.
>
> This pattern is found in all kinds of work. Farming takes the physical material of soil and seed and produces food. Music takes the physics of sound and rearranges it into something beautiful and thrilling that brings meaning to life. When we take fabric and make a piece of clothing, when we push a broom and clean up a room, when we use technology to harness the forces of electricity, when we take an unformed, naive human mind and teach it a subject, when we teach a couple how to resolve their relational disputes, when we take simple materials and turn them into a poignant work of art – we are continuing God's work of forming, filling and subduing.[11]

Whatever you got up to at work or home today, you have been in the business of fulfilling God's creation mandate by making things in this widest of senses, not just constructing objects but making

---

11 Timothy Keller, *Every Good Endeavour: Connecting Your Work to God's Work* (London: Hodder & Stoughton, 2012), p. 58.

things happen and bringing order to creation in a myriad of different ways.

This creates beauty: much-appreciated beauty in the successful reconstructive surgery, the *Bake-Off* worthy cake and the newly fitted kitchen, and underappreciated beauty creation when it comes to putting the bins out, balancing the books and coding the website.

Beauty appreciation in beauty creation

Such beauty creation is beautiful to watch. One of my favourite things in life is observing someone using the circumstances, skills and training God has given them to make things – especially things I could never do. I would pay good money to watch the carpenter who fitted my bookshelves design them, work with the grain of the wood, resolve how to cope with the lean in the floor (come to think of it, I did). Every year, I go to a local agricultural show and watch a gun dog trainer put his charges through their paces, marvelling at his intimate knowledge of each of them and the things he can make them do with just one whistle. Poet W. H. Auden (a maker of things with words) agrees with me:

> You need not see what someone is doing
> to know if it is his vocation,
>
> you only have to watch his eyes:
> a cook mixing a sauce, a surgeon
>
> making a primary incision,
> a clerk completing a bill of lading,
>
> wear the same rapt expression,
> forgetting themselves in a function.
>
> How beautiful it is,
> that eye-on-the-object look.[12]

---

12 W. H. Auden, 'Horae Canonicae: Sext', in *Selected Poems* (London: Faber & Faber, 2009), p. 227.

These are human beings doing what God has created them to do: create beauty. Watching them do that is yet another chance to appreciate beauty.

All beauty appreciation and creation involve intimacy – deeply connecting with a creature, a place or a thing. The good teacher knows their pupils well – their strengths and weaknesses, who they are. Rereading my school reports was a beautiful reminder that I had teachers who had the time and ability to get to know me well, to read me like a book. The successful winemaker knows their land well. On a recent visit to a vineyard, I was amazed at one winemaker's ability to talk about the difference between grapes grown at the top of a slope and grapes grown at the bottom. They knew the conditions, the acidity of the soil, intimately. A popular caretaker is one who knows how the heating system works as if it were part of his body. If the radiator in your room on the fifth floor isn't working, he's aware that the real problem is in the basement.

This chapter started with some words from the beginning of the poem 'Pied Beauty' by Catholic priest and poet Gerard Manley Hopkins. In it, he praises God for both the beauty he appreciates in creation (the sky, fish, trees, birds and fields) and the various jobs and tools by which we human beings create beauty alongside him. Like Manley Hopkins, we need to learn to appreciate both the beauty God has created *and* the beauty he has enabled and encouraged us to create too. That is intimacy with creation.

8
Enjoying intimacy with creation

> And isn't the whole point of things – beautiful things – that they connect you to some larger beauty? Those first images that crack your heart wide open and you spend the rest of your life chasing, or trying to recapture, in one way or another?[1]
> *Donna Tartt*

Blockers to intimacy with creation

What are the things in our lives that stop us from experiencing and producing beauty? Here are just a few of the things that can get in the way.

Ugliness

Beauty is powerful, as novelist Donna Tartt has one of her characters testify. It makes deep, lifelong connections. But some people have, tragically, experienced very little beauty in their lives.

Perhaps the place you grew up in was a soulless box on a suburban housing estate, not a home you could delight in. Perhaps the green spaces nearby were used for fly-tipping rather than nature conservation. Perhaps your parents' marriage was not attractive but abusive.

Human beings too often take potentially beautiful things – buildings, green spaces, marriages – and make them ugly in ways that discourage people from developing intimacy with creation. This is a crime against humanity because it helps to alienate people

---
1 Donna Tartt, *The Goldfinch* (Ilford: Abacus, 2014), p. 849.

from their Creator. Theologian Belden Lane is right to say that, 'It is a sin to make ugly what God has created for the purpose of reflecting and sharing God's beauty.'[2]

Christian family life is meant to be a powerful advert for God's gracious love lived out in the ups and downs of daily life, not a distorting distraction from it. Our church communities should be at the forefront of attempts to beautify or preserve the beauty of our local environments, of our natural world, so people get to enjoy God in creation. We should repent of thinking that it doesn't matter if our church buildings are ugly and/or shabby when they should be places (as much as is practically and financially possible) that showcase beautiful design, construction and art that reflects God's beauty. I'm often amazed at how much time and money some Christians will spend on furnishing their dream home while only dumping their cast-offs in their church's building.

I was recently at a Christian conference centre (that shall remain nameless) seeking to enjoy God's creation in ways that would enhance my enjoyment of God himself. But in a built environment that was so corporate and bland, it was nearly impossible to find beauty and let it point me to him. I had to head outside.

I would not have had the same problem at the Temple at Jerusalem. Its design, construction and art were deliberately beautiful. I know that we no longer need a temple, that Jesus himself is now the meeting point between God and his people (see John 2:21) and he is building a temple out of us (see Ephesians 2:21). And yet, I was thrilled to visit a friend's church building that had recently been refurbished and see that they had asked one of the best architects available to do the job beautifully. Just the design, construction and art of the staircase up to the balcony made me want to praise God.[3]

Idolatry

Human sinfulness makes beautiful things ugly and discourages people from developing intimacy with their Creator. Human

---

[2] Lane, *Ravished by Beauty*, p. 172.

[3] Quinlan Terry Architects. See pictures of the staircase at https://qtarchitects.com/projects/st-ebbes/.

sinfulness also makes beautiful things ultimate and diverts people from developing intimacy with their Creator. I've just talked about the beauty of a church building that got me praising God, but there are sadly many church buildings that people seem to worship in place of God. The Bible calls this idolatry: taking something in creation, often something especially good, and worshipping it instead of its ultimate Creator.

God's apostle Paul famously addresses this at the beginning of his letter to the Romans as he seeks to persuade every reader, Jew and Gentile, of the horror of our rejection of him:

> The wrath of God is being revealed from heaven against all the godlessness and wickedness of people, who suppress the truth by their wickedness, since what may be known about God is plain to them, because God has made it plain to them. For since the creation of the world God's invisible qualities – his eternal power and divine nature – have been clearly seen, being understood from what has been made, so that people are without excuse.
>
> For although they knew God, they neither glorified him as God nor gave thanks to him, but their thinking became futile and their foolish hearts were darkened. Although they claimed to be wise, they became fools and exchanged the glory of the immortal God for images made to look like a mortal human being and birds and animals and reptiles.
>
> Therefore God gave them over in the sinful desires of their hearts to sexual impurity for the degrading of their bodies with one another. They exchanged the truth about God for a lie, and worshipped and served created things rather than the Creator – who is for ever praised. Amen.
> (Romans 1:18–25)

Paul's point is that creation reveals God's power and divinity to us, his creatures (there are echoes of Psalm 19:1–6 here), but we ignore what it clearly tells us about him, internally suppressing the truth and externally destroying the evidence. Instead of worshipping and thanking God, we've turned our backs on him and his wisdom and become fools. We are people stupid enough to have swapped a relationship with the living and breathing Creator for the pretence of a relationship with dull and dead statues we made ourselves. God has, as a result, let us experience the consequence of a lack of intimacy with him: a lack of true intimacy with one another too, played out in wrong sexual relationships that do not satisfy. This is just one of the many consequences of us having been foolish enough to believe lies about God – we're now in the embarrassing position of spending our lives worshipping pale imitations rather than the real thing in all his glory.

This is me on the internet, searching through property porn websites and thinking that a handsome, Grade II* listed Jacobean farmhouse is the answer to all of my problems – and spending more time worshipping it, looking at photos and examining floorplans than I have spent worshipping God today.

This could be you in your idolisation of your children and their interests, the amount of money you're willing to spend on their education and entertainment so they can have opportunities denied you, which is now dwarfing the money you set aside for the building of God's kingdom. Earning enough money to pay for it all has stopped you from enjoying any intimacy with God, yourself, others or creation.

This was Augustine of Hippo, before he became a Christian, rushing around worshipping beautiful things in creation, seeking intimacy in numerous relationships and places and only belatedly turning to the source of it all. Read his famous testimony, addressed to God himself:

> Late have I loved you, beauty so old and so new: late have I loved you. And see, you were within and I was in the external world and sought you there, and in my unlovely state I plunged into those lovely created things which you made. You were with me, and I was not with you. The lovely things kept me far from you, though if they did not have their existence in you, they had no existence at all. You called and cried out loud

and shattered my deafness. You were radiant and resplendent, you put to flight my blindness. You were fragrant, and I drew my breath and now pant after you. I tasted you, and I feel but hunger and thirst for you. You touched me, and I am set on fire to attain the peace that is yours.[4]

Like him, we need to recognise our stubborn instinct to worship creation rather than our Creator. How many things good in themselves, good in their right place, have diverted our attention from him? We need to ask him to call us back to him, to come running to meet us once again, and to remind us that his beauty surpasses all others. We need to repent of allowing beautiful things to become ultimate rather than pointing us to worship the ultimate person behind them all. Intimacy with creation is only good for us if it reinforces our intimacy with him.

Not valuing this world

The danger of idolatry means that some Christians see almost everything in this world as an ungodly distraction. The best way of protecting against it is to value little in this world beyond the evangelism and discipleship that will enable you, and others, to be part of the world to come.

This was a prominent attitude among many Christians at my university. It made daily life and choices about what to do in the future very simple: everything was about rescuing people from this world for eternal life in the next one. So, a student like me – interested in politics and in making this world a better place – was diverted into what matters most: Christian ministry.

I suspect that I was no great loss to the political life of the United Kingdom. I believe that I'm spending my life well in doing the works that God has prepared in advance for me to do (which seems, coincidentally, to include a lot of church politics). But I do regret how God's creation mandate in Genesis 1:28 was completely eclipsed by the Great Commission to 'go and make disciples of

---
4 Saint Augustine, *Confessions*, p. 201.

all nations' (Matthew 28:19) in a way that I don't think that it was designed to do.

I don't think that Christians are asked to make a choice. We are to get on with the job of both caring about life in this world, this planet, *and* promoting the life of the world to come, the new heaven and new earth. This would reflect New Testament teaching, which seems to presume that Christians will continue to work for the good of this world even as we long for the arrival of the world to come (have a read of 1 Peter).

Underpinning all of this is, I think, a biblical understanding that there is a lot of continuity between this world and the next.[5] We are living in the 'shadowlands', but the shadows show us the shape of things to come *and* show us that the good we achieve in and for Christ will last. I often quote these words of Bishop Tom Wright to Christians who have been taught not to value this world and their work in it:

> What you do in the Lord *is not in vain*. You are not oiling the wheels of a machine that's about to fall over a cliff. You are not restoring a great painting that's shortly going to be thrown on the fire. You are not planting roses in a garden that's about to be dug up for a building site. You are – strange though it might seem, almost as hard to believe as the resurrection itself – accomplishing something which will become, in due course, part of God's new world. Every act of love, gratitude and kindness; every work of art or music inspired by the love of God and delight in the beauty of his creation; every minute spent teaching a severely handicapped child to read or to walk; every act of care and nurture, of comfort and support, for one's fellow human beings, and for that matter one's fellow non-human creatures; and of course every prayer, all Spirit-led teaching, every deed which spreads the gospel,

---

5 I'm aware, because I've often been surrounded by them, of those who see much more destruction and discontinuity between this world and the next. But the Bible clearly teaches restoration and continuity too, and a rebalancing towards the latter is needed in the hearts and minds of most of those I work with.

builds up the church, embraces and embodies holiness rather than corruption, and makes the name of Jesus honoured in the world – all of this will find its way, through the resurrecting power of God, into the new creation which God will one day make.[6]

Wright is using Paul's words in 1 Corinthians to encourage engagement in this world.

> Therefore, my dear brothers and sisters, stand firm. Let nothing move you. Always give yourselves fully to the work of the Lord, because you know that your labour in the Lord is not in vain.
> (1 Corinthians 15:58)

Intriguingly, these words come at the end of a chapter when Paul has been teaching about the reality of our resurrection from the dead, the Christian hope of new life in new bodies in a world made new. You might expect the application to be 'Don't worry too much about your work for Jesus in the here and now. This world will soon pass away.' But instead, it is, 'Keep going! What you do in the here and now, for God, is not a waste of time, it's not in vain because you, it, will last forever.' What we do and what we make, in this world, for Christ, is of eternal value.

Not making the time

A final block on us enjoying intimacy with creation is, for some, fuelled by not valuing this world. For others, the block is just not making the time. We like the idea of appreciating beauty and creating beauty, but we can't see how we can add it in to everything else we're trying to do.

Except that our mobile phone tells us that we did have the time to give it X number of hours last week (perhaps two digits are needed). Mine has started to do this (how?) and it has become one

---

6 Tom Wright, *Surprised by Hope* (London: SPCK, 2007), p. 219. Emphasis original.

of the most sobering moments of my week. Admittedly, some of that time was spent using it to enjoy intimacy with God (listening to music that helps me to engage with him), intimacy with myself (reading emails with some helpful feedback), and intimacy with others (arranging to meet up with friends), but very little of that time helped me to enjoy intimacy with creation in non-idolatrous ways (far too much time spent on property porn).

So, when I say that I don't have the time to go on that walk around the park and smell the roses (beauty appreciation), when I postpone taking up a creative hobby that would help me to make something (beauty creation), it's more about me reallocating my attention from an electrical box of delights to a real world that is full of much greater delights if only I would give them my proper attention. Let's turn to them now.

Catalysts for intimacy with creation

There are so many ways of enjoying intimacy with creation (delete as personally and morally appropriate): build a house or a business, plant a church or a tree, host a party or a foster child, write a play or a PhD, make a cake or a baby, watch a rugby match or a ballet, design an app or a garden, throw a pot or a cricket ball. All of these could enable you to appreciate beauty or create some beauty by helping to make a person or a thing. But let me share a couple of things I'm trying to do to grow my intimacy with creation, in the hope that they might inspire your next steps.

Walk more

While writing the first draft of this book in Cambridge, I left my faithful Honda Jazz behind in Bristol. It was so good for me to walk more (I didn't even borrow a bike in that flat, cycling city). Why? Because it slowed me down and gave me a chance to enjoy the architecture, the urban greenery and the countryside that was close by. I felt more connected to God's creation as a result. Walking to my friends' home across Grantchester Meadows helped me to appreciate the beauty of it in ways the quick journey by car would have denied me. After a day in the library staring at a screen, it was good for me to watch the evening light in the trees and appreciate the beauty of the place.

I've taken the advice of the great Ronald Blythe: 'We should cleanse our eyes in scenery – use it like lotion.'[7] That has been my experience. It could be yours too.

Enjoy poetry

Poetry also slows me down, which is one of my greatest needs in life. Normally, my eyes are rushing across the page, trying to consume words at speed, but a poem makes me take my time, work hard at understanding, feel the emotion and enjoy the connections. Poetry is one of the most intimately constructed ways of communicating, and that intimacy often ensures communication at a deeper level with greater power. As novelist John Williams puts it:

> No general ever more carefully exercises his troops in their intricate formations than does the poet dispose his words to the rigorous necessity of meter; no consul more shrewdly aligns this faction against that in order to achieve his need than the poet who balances one line with another in order to display his truth; and no Emperor ever so carefully organizes the disparate parts of the world that he rules so that they will constitute a whole than does the poet dispose the details of his poem so that another world, perhaps more real than the one that we so precariously inhabit, will spin in the universe of men's minds.[8]

The care poets take makes me take care in reading what they have written, and as I do that, I often find that they are connecting me with something in creation, myself or God that I have never really appreciated or helpfully imagined before. Just one example would be George Herbert's great poem 'Love III':

---

7 Ronald Blythe, *Next to Nature: A Lifetime in the English Countryside* (London: John Murray, 2023), p. 388.
8 John Williams, *Augustus: A Novel* (London: Vintage, 2003), p. 295.

The Intimacy Deficit

Love bade me welcome. Yet my soul drew back
    Guilty of dust and sin.
But quick-eyed Love, observing me grow slack
    From my first entrance in,
Drew nearer to me, sweetly questioning,
    If I lacked any thing.

A guest, I answered, worthy to be here:
    Love said, You shall be he.
I the unkind, ungrateful? Ah my dear,
    I cannot look on thee.
Love took my hand, and smiling did reply,
    Who made the eyes but I?

Truth Lord, but I have marred them: let my shame
    Go where it doth deserve.
And know you not, says Love, who bore the blame?
    My dear, then I will serve.
You must sit down, says Love, and taste my meat:
    So I did sit and eat.[9]

Slowing down and taking the time to work out who is speaking and what is being said, imagining what is being described and feeling the power of the last few lines, has helped me to both appreciate the beauty of a good poem and, of course, the beauty of the divine love that is being described here.

I've even started to write the odd poem myself. I'm not sure we're yet at the stage where I can honestly say they are involving me in beauty creation, but they are helping me to be more creative, slow down (again!) and enjoy intimacy in the work of creation, the careful work that John Williams describes.

---

[9] George Herbert, 'Love III'. https://www.poetryfoundation.org/poems/44367/love-iii.

Your choice

What could you do to enjoy a greater intimacy with creation? There are so many possibilities that the danger is not doing anything because we are spoiled for choice. It might be worth pausing to recall the things that have helped you to appreciate or make beauty recently – could you do that more? You could ask how your friends manage to do this in the middle of their busy lives. Or perhaps you just need to slow down while you enjoy something you already do and see how it's an act of beauty appreciation or production, and so let it connect you to the larger divine beauty that is behind all beauty everywhere.

Encouragement to intimacy with creation

I'm not sure whether any scientific research has been done on this, but John Stott maintained that 'bird watchers seldom get nervous breakdowns'.[10] Slowing down, enjoying God's creation, connecting with the beauty around us and impersonating that beauty in our creativeness is increasingly being recognised as good for our mental and physical health.

Intimacy with creation is good for our souls too. It is not an optional extra. It is not a distraction from the Christian life. It is actually one of the best things we can do to increase our intimacy with God, the most important relationship of them all. Poet Gerard Manley Hopkins was on to something when he wrote, 'I do not think I have ever seen anything more beautiful than the bluebell I have been looking at. I know the beauty of our Lord by it.'[11]

I love this example of looking at just one part of our creation, one flower, and enjoying the beauty of Jesus as a result. All intimacy

---

10 John Stott, *Challenges of Christian Leadership* (London: IVP UK, 2014), p. 37.
11 Gerard Manley Hopkins in Roger Deakin, *Wildwood: A Journey Through Trees* (London: Penguin, 2008), p. 39.

with creation should ultimately bring us back to him. Remember that beauty boomerangs.

Intimacy with creation: questions for reflection and discussion

- What is intimacy with creation?
- Why do we need to pursue it?
- What stops you from enjoying intimacy with creation?
- What could you do to enjoy it more?
- How can you make sure that happens?

Further reading

Julian Hardyman, *Maximum Life: All for the Glory of God* (London: IVP UK, 2009).

Conclusion: an intimacy audit

> We all long for unity and wholeness in life. We long for unity because we've been created for wholeness by the perfectly united triune God.[1]
> *Paul M. Gould*

Created for intimacy

I hope that, by now, you're getting your head and heart around the idea that we've been created to enjoy intimacy, a sense of unity and oneness through connection with God, ourselves, others and creation. This is, I believe, foundational to the Bible's teaching and to us living the 'life to the full' we were created to enjoy – one of wholeness, according to Christian apologist Paul Gould.

This fourfold intimacy was there at the very beginning. Listen in to biblical scholar Scot McKnight:

> Nothing in the Bible makes sense if one does not begin with the garden of Eden as a life of oneness – human beings in union with God and in communion with the self, with one another, and with the world around them. Life is about 'oneness' – oneness with God, with ourselves, with others and with the world. When the oneness is lived out, God is glorified and humans delight in that glory.[2]

---

1 Paul M. Gould, *Cultural Apologetics: Renewing the Christian Voice, Conscience, and Imagination in a Disenchanted World* (Grand Rapids, MI: Zondervan, 2019), p. 150.
2 Scot McKnight, *The Blue Parakeet: Rethinking How You Read the Bible* (Grand Rapids, MI: Zondervan, 2008), p. 71.

Conclusion

And, of course, this oneness, this communion, will be fully restored and eternally enjoyed at the very end. Read these verses from the prophecy of Isaiah about the new heaven and new earth, and spot the implicit and explicit references to intimacy with God, yourself, others and creation:

> 'See, I will create
>   new heavens and a new earth.
> The former things will not be remembered,
>   nor will they come to mind.
> But be glad and rejoice for ever
>   in what I will create,
> for I will create Jerusalem to be a delight
>   and its people a joy.
> I will rejoice over Jerusalem
>   and take delight in my people;
> the sound of weeping and of crying
>   will be heard in it no more.
> Never again will there be in it
>   an infant who lives but a few days,
>   or an old man who does not live out his years;
> the one who dies at a hundred
>   will be thought a mere child;
> the one who fails to reach a hundred
>   will be considered accursed.
> They will build houses and dwell in them;
>   they will plant vineyards and eat their fruit.
> No longer will they build houses and others live in them,
>   or plant and others eat.
> For as the days of a tree,
>   so will be the days of my people;
> my chosen ones will long enjoy
>   the work of their hands.
> They will not labour in vain,
>   nor will they bear children doomed to misfortune;
> for they will be a people blessed by the Lord,

> they and their descendants with them.
> Before they call I will answer;
>   while they are still speaking I will hear.
> The wolf and the lamb will feed together,
>   and the lion will eat straw like the ox,
>   and dust will be the serpent's food.
> They will neither harm nor destroy
>   on all my holy mountain,'
> says the LORD.
> (Isaiah 65:17–25)

Intimacy with God is here in an overwhelming abundance: he will enjoy us and anticipate our every need. Intimacy with yourself is implied: the curse is gone, work is now enjoyed and there is no more mourning, crying or pain. Intimacy with others is promised: God's people are united, and death no longer separates us from our loved ones. Intimacy with creation is included: building and planting continues but without frustration, and all God's creatures live together in perfect harmony.

American artist Horace Pippin has painted this final scene in his wonderful *Holy Mountain III*. A print hangs in my study and helps me to look forward to this happy day.

A sense of oneness through connection – fullness through relationship with God, yourself, others and creation – was there in the very beginning. We will enjoy it fully in the future, but the challenge for us now is to make it as much a part of our present experience as we possibly can.

An intimacy audit

This is where the intimacy audit I trailed in the introduction comes in. It is not the most exciting or sophisticated of tools; it's just a way of assessing how much of an intimacy deficit there is in your life by using the questions below to note the signs of intimacy there are and the potential solutions for any lack of it you see or feel. I use these questions a lot in the pastoral conversations I have with others, to check in with friends, and to assess how I'm doing myself. Sometimes, I draw the table below and work through it; at other times it's just in my mind, shaping the things I'm asking and what I'm saying to others (or myself). I've found that whatever the presenting issues – broken relationships, painful loneliness, powerful addictions, crippling anxieties – help will be found in registering what intimacy is missing, talking, and praying through how the deficit can best be filled. It is not a silver bullet, and I point people to other places for help (counselling, their doctor, addiction support groups, CBT), but completing an intimacy audit has always helped in some shape or form.

My intimacy audit

Let me attempt to demonstrate how these questions help by carrying out an audit of the intimacy deficit in my life today.

Intimacy with God

What intimacy with God am I enjoying? There are encouraging signs of me enjoying an increasing intimacy, a felt connectedness, with God. Adopting Psalm 23 over recent years has been so enriching. Its words and images keep connecting me to God in

Table 1: The intimacy audit

Intimacy with God	Intimacy with Yourself
What intimacy with God am I enjoying?	What intimacy with self am I enjoying?
How could I enjoy it more?	How could I enjoy it more?
Intimacy with Others	**Intimacy with Creation**
What intimacy with others am I enjoying?	What intimacy with creation am I enjoying?
How could I enjoy it more?	How could I enjoy it more?

a whole host of different circumstances and emotions. Similarly, time spent dwelling on the reality of God as my loving Father has been good for me – exploring the parable of the prodigal son in the company of writers like Henri Nouwen[3] and Tim Keller[4] has been a catalyst for intimacy and helpful in recognising the things that so often stop me from feeling the Father love of God. Writing and speaking on the relationship between Christ and the church as the ultimate marriage has been life changing too.[5]

How could I enjoy intimacy with God more? All of that said, I limit my sense of connection by not talking to God enough. I wish I would run to him more instinctively when I'm pleased or distressed, as a young child does with their parents. I'd love to remember and act as if he is with me always, a constant friend in all circumstances. It would be good if my day started and ended with me chatting to him, as spouses might do in bed.

I need to pray that I'd pray more. I need to ask others to join in praying that I would and ask them to pray with me to help me along. I need to spend time in parts of Scripture that will further embed the reality of God as our Father, friend and fiancé in my life. Adopting some other psalms might help. I could let, for instance, the intimacy of Psalm 45 deepen my connection with God as I do with it everything I've already done with Psalm 23.

Intimacy with yourself

What intimacy with self am I enjoying? I have a much better sense of my strengths and weaknesses than I did a few years back. Both the church and the charity I work for have started having the sort of conversations that enable this to happen, helping to develop the sort of right humility that can say what I can and cannot do. Recent time away on holiday and study leave (to write this book)

---

[3] Henri J. M. Nouwen, *The Return of the Prodigal Son: A Story of Homecoming* (London: Darton, Longman and Todd, 1994).

[4] Timothy Keller, *The Prodigal God: Recovering the Heart of the Christian Faith* (London: Viking Press, 2008).

[5] Ed Shaw, *Purposeful Sexuality: A Short Christian Introduction* (London: IVP UK, 2021).

has reminded me of how much I love the roles God has given me – and how well they fit me – in a way that has made me feel not just disconnected from them but disconnected from myself when I'm away.

How could I enjoy intimacy with myself more? I do need to recognise, as life gets busier and I get older, that I've been created with limits. I need to have properly policed boundaries if I'm to be the person who God has created me to be effectively – especially in a godly way and not some ungodly parody. With the help of others, I need to work out a sustainable way of being me.

I need to share with others how much busyness takes it out of me and those times when their desire for me to do something is going to undermine me eventually. I think that I need to become more aware of both the strengths and weaknesses God has uniquely given me and lean into them. I'm a capable generalist in many ways, but that is killing me as I'm asked to do too many things. I need to be asking myself and others, 'Am I uniquely placed to do this?' If not, God might need to provide someone else.

Intimacy with others

What intimacy with others am I enjoying? I've been blessed with a wide circle of friends. I thank God for each of them. But in recent years, I've recognised that attempting (and failing) to keep up with them all has sometimes meant that there is no inner circle of friends who really know how I'm doing, what's going on inside. There has been an intimacy deficit. I've recently been more intentional in making time for a particular few, and that has made a huge difference to me (and, I hope, to them). Again, being away from Bristol for a couple of months has underlined how important they have become to me through the lack of much recent time with them.

How could I enjoy intimacy with others more? I'm doing better on intentionality, but probably not on constancy. Busyness and time away undermine intimacy in my friendships because I'm not around enough. I also need to open up to a few more people and widen the 'inner circle' (if I can put it like that) so I don't become too dependent on just a few and can benefit from what different people can bring. A friend who brought real intergenerational depth into my life recently died. She is irreplaceable, but perhaps it's now time for me to think about offering what she gave me to someone in a younger generation.

So I need to give some time to thinking about whom I might befriend and connect more with. I need to limit the time I spend away, or make sure that I'm still in touch with key people in my life when I am. As soon as I'm back in Bristol after writing this book, I need to get the diary out and book in the times when I'm going to see people. But alongside intentionality, I need to make sure that I embrace spontaneity in friendships, making time for things that haven't been in the diary for months, or new friendships that God has decided would do me good.

Intimacy with creation

What intimacy with creation am I enjoying? Recent time away has, positively, enabled me to appreciate the beauty of Herm as the sun rises and of Grantchester Meadows as the sun sets. In the last few weeks, I've also enjoyed God's creation in a walled garden, at the cinema, in an art gallery and through some good books. I've caught up with two of my godchildren, seen all of my nephews and nieces and invested in the next generation. I hope that I've been making something useful in this book.

How could I enjoy intimacy with creation more? When I head home, the danger is that I will return to a largely sedentary, indoor life. I will be back in my car, rushing everywhere and not slowing down to enjoy God's creation. I need to re-examine the amount of time I spend on my phone, recognising that it's a constant distraction that eats up time that could be better used reading a poem, admiring a view or walking around the block.

Potential solutions include walking into work some days, taking the time to enjoy my city and slow down a bit. I also need to get out of the city more and visit the National Trust properties near Bristol. The poetry books need to be read as well as bought. Perhaps I should stop talking about taking up a creative hobby and sign up for a course in the autumn? When my idols distract me from worshipping God, I need to both repent of them and recall how he alone provides what I think I'll get from them.

A virtuous cycle

As soon as you begin to do a detailed intimacy audit like this, you'll begin to see how greater intimacy in one area can produce, or is dependent upon, intimacy in another. I feel most connected to God when I'm most connected with creation. I've felt more at one with myself, more aware of my strengths and weaknesses, when other people have helped me to see what they are. It's other people who have most helped me to grasp what God's creation mandate is all about and what it means to create beauty in this world. And it's beauty that brings me back to worship God again – back around the virtuous cycle we go.

As a result, one or two changes in life will help to make up an intimacy deficit in all four areas. If I restarted the mentoring of younger Christians that I used to give so much time to, it would increase my intimacy with God (I best understand and appreciate his word in the company of others), my intimacy with myself (it gives me a context in which to share my strengths and weaknesses), my intimacy with others (it builds a new friendship) and intimacy with creation (it's a way in which I can get involved in producing, making and shaping the next generation).

Walking more would also cut the intimacy deficit in every part of the quadrant. It would see me connect more with God, as I pray best while out walking. It would connect me better with myself, as I used my body and felt its strength and weakness. It would connect me with others, as I asked them to join me on a walk. It would connect me with creation, as I slowed down to enjoy it properly.

So doing some mentoring and walking might be the best way to cut the intimacy deficit in my life. It won't disappear totally until

Conclusion

the new heaven and new earth, but in the meantime, those might be two very practical things that I can get on and do – noting how both of them could also help to lessen the intimacy deficit in other people's lives.

What about you?

Do your own intimacy audit. How much of an intimacy deficit are you experiencing? In which of the areas are you feeling it most? Are there any obvious solutions? Why not use the results to start a conversation with a good friend and get their input? Just doing that will, no doubt, begin to deepen your connection with them. Talking about intimacy breeds intimacy.

The huge potential

If everyone who read this book did a similar intimacy audit and came up with a couple of simple changes they could make, I suspect that the pastoral impact on us all would be great. I'm not saying that all broken relationships, painful loneliness, powerful addictions, crippling anxieties and the rest would end overnight, but I think that they could be considerably lessened. We were created to need intimacy, and the lack of it is fuelling each of these things. If we cut the deficit, it would have a massive positive impact on us all.

Cutting the intimacy deficit would impact the watching world too. Because all human beings were created to enjoy intimacy, those outside of the church are experiencing the intimacy deficit too – often in deeper and more painful ways.

When we talk about Christianity, we should be appealing to people's deep sense of wanting to be connected and united with something, someone, greater than themselves – as well as connected to themselves, other people and the world around them. We need to become better at helping people to see how everything they rightly desire will only be satisfied in the relational intimacy the gospel makes possible through Jesus.

Jesus the intimacy giver

We are only able to reduce the intimacy deficit in the here and now because of Jesus: his life, death and resurrection make reconciliation and reconnection possible with God, ourselves, others and creation. He is at the centre of any virtuous cycle of intimacy in our lives, and one day soon, everyone who has trusted in him will fully feel that reality and will no longer experience any intimacy deficit. Instead, we will be united and whole, fully enjoying oneness through connection with God, ourselves, others and creation forever.

For as Jesus says to us:

> I have come that they may have life, and have it to the full.
> (John 10:10)

And as Jesus prays for us:

> My prayer is not for them alone. I pray also for those who will believe in me through their message, that all of them may be one, Father, just as you are in me and I am in you. May they also be in us so that the world may believe that you have sent me.
> (John 17:20–21)

Amen.

Acknowledgements

This book was first commissioned by IVP back in 2018. The patience of Eleanor Trotter, then Caleb Woodbridge, and now Tom Creedy and Joshua Wells (my editor) has been more than I deserve. My thanks to them all.

The long germination period of this book has allowed me to experiment with its contents on many, including a church weekend away for St John's Church in Yeovil, a men's retreat for Sterling Park Baptist Church in Virginia, the True Freedom Trust's annual conference, and numerous different contexts across the Emmanuel Bristol family of churches. Huge thanks to all who provided both critical feedback and timely encouragement, especially the wonderful Ellie Maffett, who helped me to run a whole 'Intimacy Day' here in Bristol.

The trustees of Emmanuel Bristol and *Living Out* were kind in granting me a month's study leave to finally write what I'd been delaying for far too long. I'm grateful for their prayerful and financial support for a month at Tyndale House in Cambridge. There, I was made to feel welcome by the staff and other occupants of the soon-to-be demolished library (I'm looking forward to returning and using the new one). Friends in Cambridge were good at inviting me out for meals and (just about) preserving my sanity levels as I tried to churn out between one and two thousand words a day. Friends in Bristol helped by sending me flowers and café vouchers. Friends from all over are part of the 'Ed Shaw Prayer Support' messaging group, who respond prayerfully to my regular cries for help. Thanks all.

Friends and colleagues at Emmanuel and *Living Out* have covered for me so I could both trial and write the contents of this book. At my church (Emmanuel City Centre), I'm especially

Acknowledgements

grateful to Mike Harris for everything he enables me to do elsewhere by being such a fantastic fellow pastor. My church family are the good company in which I'm most learning to put this book into practice myself. I love you all.

I'm blessed with wonderful family and friends. Special thanks go to those who provided feedback on the first main draft: Adam, Alasdair, Andrew, Andy, Dan, Hannah, Hazel, Helen, Hilary, Jo, Phil, Simon, Steve and the anonymous IVP intern. Reading through each of your comments was so helpful. I hope that you're encouraged to see your impact on the final edition and will forgive any times when your input was rudely ignored. All the remaining faults are, of course, my own.

Kind supporters have paid for me to have a part-time assistant for much of the last ten years. I'm grateful to them and to those who have been willing to be my carers: Millie, Hannah, Dan and Steve. Steve has been especially helpful in getting this book off my desk – finally!

My dear honorary aunt Ruth Kisch died just before I started my study leave. She permeates the pages of this book because we talked so much about its contents over the past fifteen years. Her constant love and prayers have been such an important, and now much missed, part of my life.

My older nephew and nieces have been dropping unsubtle hints for a while that they would like to appear in a book by me. So, this one is dedicated to them with the hope that it might, one day, do each of them some good, as their presence in my life does me so much good. I love them more than words can ever say.

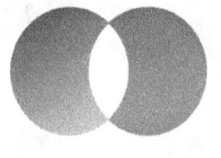

Living Out

We help people, churches and society talk about faith and sexuality.

livingout.org

www.ingramcontent.com/pod-product-compliance
Lightning Source LLC
Chambersburg PA
CBHW070202100426
42743CB00013B/3014